SECRET BARS & RESTAURANTS IN PARIS

SECRET BARS & RESTAURANTS IN PARIS

Jacques Garance
Photography Stéphanie Rivoal

Jonglez

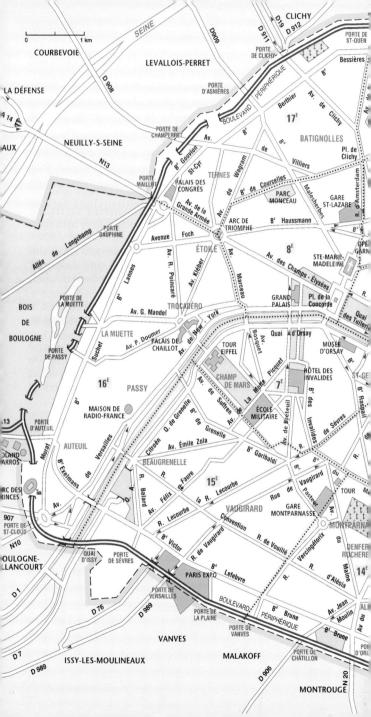

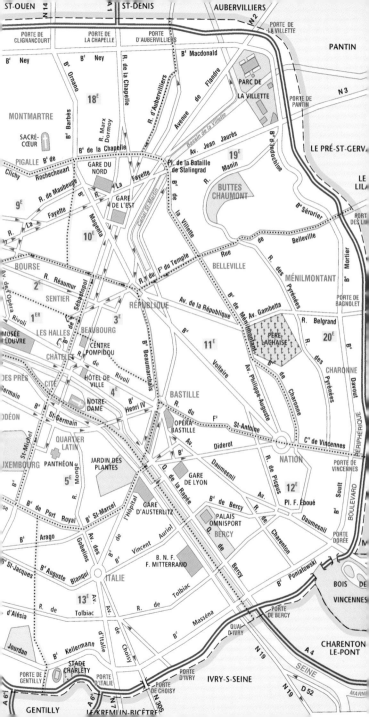

TABLE OF CONTENTS

MAIN PLACES

THEMES

CAFÉS RICHELIEU, MOLLIEN ET DENON

Musée du Louvre 75001 Paris
• Access : métro Palais-Royal - Musée du Louvre
• Open daily except Tuesdays, 10am-5pm (9pm Mon & Wed)
• Café Denon. Open daily except Tuesdays, 9am-5pm (7pm Mon & Wed)

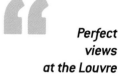

*Perfect
views
at the Louvre*

Of course, you'll first need to buy a ticket to enter the Louvre itself. This will give you a chance to discover parts of the museum that have hitherto escaped your notice. And don't say that you've already seen it all, because no one will believe you.

Among its numerous eating and drinking venues, the Louvre has three cafés with such exceptional views that self-respecting Parisians find it difficult to abandon them wholly to the tourists. But most inhabitants of the French capital don't even know they exist. These unique cafés all have, each in their own style, terraces that should not be missed.

Located, as its name indicates, in the Richelieu wing of the museum, the Café Richelieu has a terrace looking southward, ideal for lazing in the sun while perusing the newspaper amidst the rare tourists who have stumbled upon it, unaware of their luck. From this vantage point, sheltered from the pollution and the noise, the view takes in the pyramid and the Denon wing, and further to the right, the beginning of the Tuileries gardens and the Eiffel Tower. Sitting at one of the forty tables, you should simply order a cold drink as the food here consists mainly of snacks and some rather mediocre sandwiches. In fact, it's a shame that tourists are given such a poor impression of France in a place like the Louvre….

Diametrically opposed to this first café, on the far side of the pyramid, the Café Mollien offers similar attractions, but without the sunshine. Perfect for hot summer days…

The most secret of the three is without a doubt the Café Denon. In the museum wing bearing the same name, look for the Roman Egypt room that leads to the café. Smile when you reach the reception, and then go on through the French windows straight in front of you. You'll find yourself in a little hidden paradise. Sit down at one of the five tables and take in the surroundings. There's a little lawn, a few trees, and a small fountain whose tinkling is guaranteed to immediately calm the nerves. Sheer bliss. You have just found your way into the Cour Denon, one of least-known inner courtyards within the Louvre. It's an open-air annex to the more famous Cour Marly, and possesses a magnificent horseshoe-shaped staircase, which in fact once allowed access by horseback to the Salle de Manège above. The little café terrace is situated within the arms of the horseshoe. Unfortunately, the heavy hand of bureaucracy prevents a lady or gentleman of your refined tastes from lunching here. Make do with a cold drink, since the café's fare is of poor quality.

CERCLE SUÉDOIS

242, rue de Rivoli 75001 Paris
• Access: M° Concorde
• Tel.: 01 42 60 76 67
• www.cercle-suedois.com
• Open to the public the first and last Wednesdays of every month, 5pm-9pm

Swedish chic

Marvellous! Twice each month, only two steps away from the place de la Concorde, the highly secret and elegant Cercle Suedois, founded in 1891, welcomes readers of this guide for a very exclusive evening.

From the street, a discreet plaque indicates the existence of a Swedish and Norwegian club. Go up to the second floor, open the door on the right, and you're there. At the reception, the high-spirited Gunilla Poulet collects your contribution of €8 permitting you to spend an astonishing evening there. To the right after the entrance, a grand salon in a classic style features a lively professional jazz band. Louise Angerman, the dynamic and friendly manager of this very select club, even sings on occasion, in English.

Behind the musicians, a door opens into a historic room: it was here, on 27 November 1895 and upon a desk that still remains in its original spot, that

Alfred Nobel, the inventor of dynamite, drafted his equally explosive will establishing the famous Nobel Prizes.

Lastly, just next door, one finds an English-style bar which is a much-favoured meeting-place for Swedish expatriates and French Swedophiles. The selection of vodkas and beers available explains the often jovial state of the highly distinguished members in their impeccable suits and ties. The general atmosphere, out of another era, is a delight for visiting aesthetes and those who enjoy off-beat surroundings. The walls are adorned with numerous canvasses by Swedish artists, including Zorn, Grünewald, Dardel, and more recently, Lennart Jirlow. To make the evenings flow pleasantly, the club members and their guests are extremely approachable, and one soon finds oneself chatting with everyone.

FOYER CONCORDE

restaurant associatif polonais de la crypte de notre-dame-de-l'assomption

Place Maurice-Barrès and 263 bis, rue Saint-Honoré 75001 Paris
- Tel.: 01 42 60 43 33
- Access: M° Concorde or Madeleine
- Open daily lunch time and evenings, except on Mondays

Catholic Poland

Lost in the middle of place Maurice-Barrès is a sign indicating to anyone who, by accident, happens to read it, the presence nearby of a Polish restaurant in the crypt of the Notre-Dame-de-l'Assomption church.

Located in the vaulted 17th century cellars, the restaurant is a veritable oddity. Having descended the few short steps leading to the crypt, the atmosphere of the place takes you by surprise. A long stone hallway accommodates ten tables, presided over by a crucifix lodged in an alcove at the far end, while the musical accompaniment alternates between Polish pop and Western techno. Very strange, indeed.

You're given a brisk welcome by a waitress, Polish, of course, with little time to waste and who knows her business, making it quite clear that she will in no way be intimidated by any blustering from the likes of you. So, you quickly take a look at the menu.

There are Polish specialities, vodkas, some East European wines from Slovenia and Hungary, and you soon realize just exactly where you've landed.

Surprisingly, after a fairly brief wait - as you'd expect given the speed shown by the aforementioned waitress - you find the dish in front of you to be good, even very good. All of it for a modest price: individual dishes range from €8 to €18, lunch menus from €10.90 to €15.60 (€29 to €35 in the evenings). It's very reasonable for the quality.

And when it's hot outside, the coolness of the crypt is particularly pleasant.

After your meal, spend a few quiet moments in the church overhead, thanking the Lord for having been fed so well. And if you've really fallen under the spell, linger awhile on the porch out front to read the posters on the façade and find out where you can catch a bus bound for Poland !

FOOTSIE

12, rue Daunou 75002 Paris
• Access: M° Opéra
• Open from 12noon-4pm and 6pm-2am (4am on Fri & Sat)

Alcoholic Stock Exchange

Here's an astonishing concept adopted by Benjamin Schindler when he opened this bar-restaurant in March 2001. Inspired by an idea already successfully put into practice in Germany, Spain, England, Belgium and Luxemburg, the proprietor decided to vary the price of drinks in accord with demand. Using stock exchange software, the system, for example, varies the price of a beer from €3 to €7, whisky from €6 to €11, and a glass of champagne from €6 to €12… To order, watch closely one of the four plasma screens that display drink prices, but be quick about it: the prices only stay valid for four minutes. So if you are about to order an Amstel at €3.50, you'll need to beat out the band of drunks standing behind you before they order a round of ten and immediately boost the price to €5. But to prevent, for example, that Amstel from remaining at an absurdly high price for too long, three times a night there's

a stock market crash when all the prices fall. That's the time to grab firm hold of the nearest waiter and give him your order.

To add to the appeal, the staff are friendly and the venue itself is attractive, with warm wood panelling and a comfortable amount of space, where you can also have a simple meal.

Note that the variable prices of drinks does not apply at lunch time. And just in case you don't know, Footsie is the nickname of the London Financial Times Stock Exchange (FTSE) index, and thus the equivalent of the CAC 40 in Paris or the Dow Jones in New York.

RAIDD BAR

23, rue du Temple 75003 Paris
- Access: M° Rambuteau
- www.raiddbar.com
- Open daily 5pm-2am

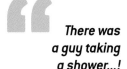

There was a guy taking a shower...!

If those of you seeking the unusual could only visit just one gay bar in the Marais neighbourhood, it should be the Raidd Bar. As opposed to the others, the Raidd Bar is not merely a meeting-place or a pickup joint for homosexuals.

Every evening at 8.30pm, 9.30pm, 10.30pm and 11.30pm, a handsome, but above all, perfectly proportioned young man actually takes his shower before the watchful eyes of the excited crowd.

Protected by a wall of glass from any eventual urges to touch, it's all there: the showerhead, the water that really runs, the bar of soap that our man takes sly pleasure in running sensually over his entire body. Only his genitals remain invisible, as modesty but above all the law requires.

But except for the virile member which is only hinted at, being draped in a towel that just barely remains decent, you get to see everything. The buttocks press conspicuously against the glass and the hand of course lingers deliberately at the most lubricious spots, offering the perfect show for the Marais scene : the bar is packed every evening.

For those who haven't had their eyeful yet, it's time to go down to the loo in the cellar. Place yourself calmly in front of one of the urinals available.

Look straight in front of you. A video screen is facing back at you. Taking a closer look and you'll see a partial view of yourself. This is the right moment for some young Adonis to decide to use the urinal opposite. Stand still, looking straight ahead. Surprise! The video screen gives you the refreshing impression that the young Adonis in question is watching you intently... But rest assured, he'll be getting the same impression on his side...

Accessible to curious women, too, but only if (properly) accompanied.

CAFÉ-BAR LES TEMPLIERS

35, rue de Rivoli 75004 Paris
• Access: M° Hôtel-de-Ville
• Tel.: 01 42 72 00 07
• Open daily 6am-2am

**In the name
of the King**

From the outside, Les Templiers is one of the French capital's countless PMU (licensed betting) cafés, without any character other than offering its regular customers somewhere to partake of their small glass of white wine at 9am in the morning.

But once inside, it's a different story. Every square centimetre of wall surface is covered with statues, photos, portraits, paintings, and objects of all sorts whose common denominator is the fact that they sing the praises of the kings of France and their present-day descendants. Les Templiers is the only Royalist bar in Paris and proud of it. Jacques Serre, the current proprietor, simply kept the café's name, bequeathed by the previous owner. Hence the medieval order of the Templars now finds itself curiously associated with French royalty. An astounding allusion when one recalls that Louis XVI was held in the Temple prison before being beheaded…

On ordinary days, leaning on the bar in front of your beer, your attention will thus oscillate between this strange little Royalist museum and the

bettors who are far more excited about the results of their horses in the races than by portraits of the Comte de Paris, the current heir to the French throne.

All this changes on the nights of 20-21 January and 16-17 October. These are respectively the anniversaries of the deaths of Louis XVI and of Marie-Antoinette, the major dates when French royalists gather together.

For the more fanatical supporters of the cause, beside the cigarette counter there is a small display case which, in addition to the inevitable Zippos and cigar cutters, offers a range of unusual and appealing royalist mementoes.

DANS LE NOIR

51, rue Quincampoix 75004 Paris
- Access: RER Châtelet-Les Halles
- Tel.: 01 42 77 98 04
- Open Mon-Sat. 3 services daily: 12.30pm, 8pm, and 10pm
- Brunch on Sundays, 12noon-5pm
- Open daily 5.30pm-7.30pm, then midnight-2am
- Surprise menu: €21 to €35

Pitch Black

We provide a playful, sensorial, and human adventure, perhaps a little « crazy, but that's exactly why it should work. It has already existed in Zurich and Berlin for several years now,» says Edouard de Broglie, instigator of the project. The idea is that of dining in complete darkness, guided throughout by blind persons who take on the role of waiters for the occasion. It's an exceptional way of living an extraordinary experience, but also and above all, for a short while, of putting yourself in the shoes of a blind person and hence better understanding, very concretely, the real nature of their handicap.

Depending on the diners, a discussion may strike up with your host or hostess for the evening, allowing them a chance to raise the awareness of the wider public, but also giving them more contact with sighted people, not always as frequent as it might seem… The evening begins at the cloakroom, where you are supposed to leave any object capable of emitting even a little light: lighters, watches, mobile phones….

So darkness really will be total. The same rule applies to the organizers who, one evening, served sushi that turned out to be fluorescent in the dark!

Shortly after, a blind waiter or waitress arrives to take guests by the hand and guide them to their seats. That's when things start in earnest. When you have to pour wine in your glass, or try stabbing your food with your fork…

Whether you have your eyes open or shut, it makes no difference. It's pitch black! Soon, conversations get going as questions begin to gush forth: 'Is there apple in this?…' It's only on the way out, when you get a chance to read the actual composition of the surprise menu, that you come to realize the degree to which we are all conditioned by the sight of food…

During dinner, you find yourself touching the shoulder or arm of another customer… although you're just looking for your glass or your plate….

Tuesday evenings are even reserved for singles; this venue is clearly a winner for fans of 'blind dates'! Only one negative note: the dining room is very noisy, because people talk much louder when they can't see! The food is quite decent, but in any case not the real reason for coming here.

BEL CANTO

72, quai de l'Hôtel-de-Ville 75004 Paris
- Access: M° Hôtel-de-Ville or Pont-Marie
- Tel.: 01 42 78 30 18
- Open daily from 8pm

6, rue du Commandant-Pillot 92200 Neuilly-sur-Seine
- Access: M° Sablon or Porte-Maillot
- Tel.: 01 47 47 19 94
- Open Tues-Sat from 8pm
- Lunch Mon-Fri, without opera

88, rue de la Tombe-Issoire 75014 Paris
- Access: M° Alésia
- Tel.: 01 43 22 96 15
- Open Tues-Sat from 8pm
- Dinner & show: €60

*Operatic
waiters*

The concept? Delicious Italian cuisine served by waiters who sing opera. Imagine yourself in a red-and-gold decor with balconies, balustrades, and a grand piano. You are sitting at a table covered with a lace cloth, looking at the opera posters on the wall and the mannequins wearing costumes from the Opéra National de Paris. Bought at the auction organized by the Paris Opéra in October 1999, there's the embroidered vest of Count Almaviva (from the 1973 season), displayed alongside the costume of William Tell (1969), the jacket of Romeo and Juliet's gown (1956).

A waiter arrives, takes your order, and then suddenly transforms himself into Rigoletto or Figaro. He's soon joined by a quartet of young singers (soprano, mezzo soprano, tenor, and baritone).

At first you're surprised, then enchanted…

Next, they all go back to waiting on you, asking you to choose between the pasta in squid's ink and the trio de Parme.

Every evening, a troupe of young singers, most of them students from various Paris conservatories, take part in this entertainment by performing the greatest arias of opera. The programme includes Verdi, Mozart, Puccini, Rossini…

It's a pure delight for lovers of lyrical art, and of Italian food.

Inaugurated at Hôtel-de-Ville in 2000, the restaurant's concept has worked so well that Jacques de la Bussière, the proprietor, has since opened other branches in the 14th arrondissement in 2001 and in Neuilly in September 2004.

LA TABLE DES GOURMETS

14, rue des Lombards 75004 Paris
• Access: M° Hôtel-de-Ville or Châtelet-Les Halles
• Open daily lunch time and evenings, except on Sundays
• Menus from € 15

Dine in a 12th century chapel

Just a short walk from Les Halles, at the very heart of the tourist district in the centre of Paris, the Table des Gourmets will be a very pleasant surprise even to many Parisians. Those of you looking for a meal after seeing a play at the Théâtre de la Ville or the Théâtre du Châtelet won't regret dining here.

You may be perplexed upon arriving. The big room on the ground floor doesn't look like much. Don't worry, just go on downstairs. In the cellar, the restaurant occupies a magnificent, medieval-looking room with high, vaulted ceilings. This room is none other than a historic 12th century chapel, where pilgrims about to make the long journey by foot to Santiago de Compostela listened to sermons. The nearby Saint-Jacques tower is also associated with this famous pilgrimage.

In this truly spectacular and surprising decor, the French cuisine is simple but good and the fixed menu of starter-main course-dessert for €15 at lunch or dinner is quite satisfactory.

Curiously run by a Chinese family for the past fifteen years - no egg or spring rolls on the menu, but instead bavette à l'échalotte and avocados with cocktail sauce - the restaurant caters above all to regulars as well as Asian friends of the owners. The service is thoughtful, attentive, and efficient.

TEATIME & TALKTIME - CHEZ MICKAEL

- Tel: 01 43 25 86 55
- Every Saturday at 5pm
- €10 per person

Take tea at the home of a perfect stranger

A little bit like Jim Haynes who has complete strangers come over to his place for dinner, Michaël, a nice guy now in his fifties, came up about eight years ago with the excellent idea of inviting new faces to take tea in his home.

Start by calling him. After a brief chat, he will give you his address, plus his building access code, and soon you'll find yourself, along with fifty other people, in a very pleasant Parisian flat in the 5th arrondissement.

After making a 'gift' of €10 per person to cover costs, and perhaps a little extra for Michaël's sake, you have a cup of tea because after all you did come here for that! But, if like most of the other guests, you are really just interested in meeting some new people, you won't be disappointed.

With a range of ages from 25 on up to around 50, a good half of those attending are foreigners. Ukrainian students looking for fun, New Zealander expats, the odd Venezuelan artist and some French people thrown in to add body, there's a little of everything, and that's all to the good.

Ideal for foreigners who have just arrived in Paris, for Parisians who want to open their horizons, and for those seeking company, Michaël's flat is sort of a living melting-pot that's all too rare in Paris.

Officially, you're supposed to speak French during the first half of the proceedings (which last until around 8 to 8.30pm), then any other language you please thereafter…

CHEZ MAÏ

65, rue Galande 75005 Paris
- Access: M° Saint-Michel or Cluny-La Sorbonne
- Tel.: 01 43 54 05 33
- Open daily, lunch time and evenings
- About € 10 per person
- Cheques and credit cards not accepted

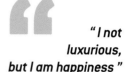

" I not luxurious, but I am happiness "

Chez Maï is an absolutely unique restaurant, beyond time or fashion, whose delights you should hurry to sample, most notably the personality of its Vietnamese owner who gave her name to the establishment.

Maï, now aged 75, is a small, lively woman full of humour who lends the place all her charm.

There's barely room here for three tables, plus a fourth, but the latter is devoted to odds and ends carefully arranged by Maï: all sorts of boxes, empty or full, broken lamps, and a few old books. Once seated, take your time and enjoy the entertainment: after welcoming you and bringing the menus, Maï goes back to her own seat to watch television, which is always turned on. A little window gives you a glimpse of the owner's merry face, as she concentrates on her game show. So concentrated in fact that she actively takes part, standing up to take her measuring tape, imagining a measure, and announcing the answer out loud to the television set. Then she interrupts herself to come take your order. 'Everything is good,' she declares, '…if you like …'.

And it's true, everything is good. The nems (€3.50) are crispy and delicious, while the main dishes, at the unbeatable prices of €4.50 or €5.50 for the most expensive, also hit the mark. Even the coconut cake at €1 is good, as is rarely the case in an Asian restaurant.

And for the same price, while you sit before your plastic tablecloth, back against the plywood wall, you receive a lesson in life. That of a woman who arrived in France in 1968 after fleeing the Communist regime in Vietnam and has obviously not had an easy time of it, but who managed to open this place in 1988. She won't be voting for the Communist party in the next elections, she confides, but she takes the right to vote seriously, coming from a country where people have fought and died quite recently to obtain it.

The lesson ends with a sublime, 'I not luxurious, but I am happiness,' as she leaves you with an immense smile on her face.

Be sure to visit soon, Maï won't last forever.

LE PARLOIR CHRÉTIEN

9, rue du Vieux-Colombier 75006 Paris
- Access: M° Saint-Sulpice
- Tel.: 01 45 48 30 34
- Open Wed-Sat 12.15pm-7.30pm, and Sundays 4pm-7pm

> *A special atmosphere of togetherness and sharing*

Established fourteen years ago, the Parloir Chrétien, or 'Parloir du Colombier' (Dovecote Parlour), is a truly timeless place. Located in the middle of the Saint-Sulpice neighbourhood with its trendy boutiques and pretty girls, the Parloir offers a breather from a busy day where you can spend a quiet moment in a very special atmosphere of togetherness and sharing.

In a wooden decor that almost reminds one of an Alpine chalet, the Parloir's main adornments, if one may use the term, are a statue of the Virgin Mary along with those of several saints. Facing the entrance is a photo of the Pope that gives the impression of greeting each visitor. And next to John Paul II there's a handsome miniature reproduction in wood of the Milan cathedral that catches one's eye.

As for the staff, if once again one is allowed to use the term, they are made up of volunteers who donate a little of their time to the service of a venue

for meeting and listening to others. A priest is there every afternoon to enter into dialogue with those who desire this. Magazines are available: Pèlerinage, Famille chrétienne… You can also obtain a supporter's card for €25 and receive the 'Le Colombier' bulletin with news about the Parloir. But the Parloir is also a friendly place where you can eat and drink at very Christian prices: €1 for a large glass of lemonade, €4 for a quiche with salad, €2 for tea and for desserts. Hard to beat. For those who want to give into the sin of gluttony, don't miss their almond cake, home-made as is all the food on sale.

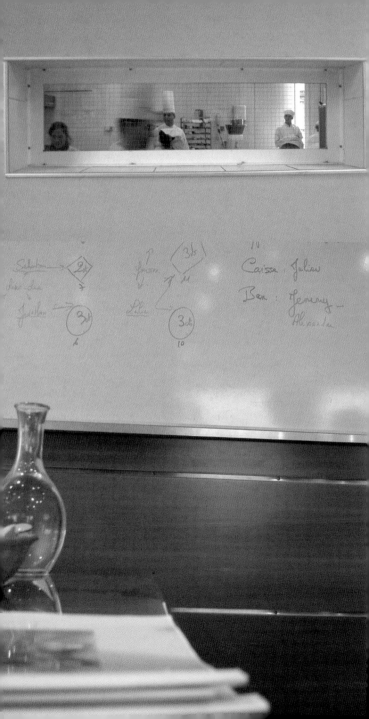

ÉCOLE GRÉGOIRE-FERRANDI

28, rue de l'Abbé-Grégoire 75006 Paris
- Access: M° Saint-Placide, Sèvres-Babylone or Vaneau
- Open weekdays at lunch time and Thursday evenings
- Menus: €18, €22, and €35
- Reservations, call 01 49 54 17 31 and ask for Mme Hatchi, Mon-Fri 8am-5pm

***Student
exploitation***

One of a series of restaurants run by the French hostelry schools, this is the founding father, that is, the oldest of them all. From the street, there isn't a sign or a blackboard that indicates the existence of this restaurant which is nevertheless open to the public. Only the students gathered at the school's entrance draw your attention. When you enter, turn right immediately, pass in front of the reception, keep going, take the lift up to the fourth floor (hence the original name of the restaurant…), and you're there. A long hallway leads to the dining room. Alongside it, a window reveals the students busy in the kitchens, adding a touch of industrial cuisine ambience.

Generally somewhat advanced in years, the restaurant's regular clientele has latched onto a good thing: for the price of a quick lunch in any ordinary Parisian bistro, customers are served a superb meal. This unequalled value for money is due to the very nature of the restaurant. All of the waiters and cooks are unpaid students. There are no wage costs, but no advertising allowed, either, or else other restaurants simply could not compete on equal terms.

So, if you have the time, like the numerous pensioners who tend to gather here, come enjoy the delicious provincial atmosphere, a fascinating mix of formality offset by the earnest amateurism of the waiters, an elegant but somewhat dated decor, and a maître d'hôtel-instructor who trains his pupils with a deadpan sense of humour, and obviously a favourite confidant of the amused customers.

On Mondays and Fridays, there's a fixed menu costing €18 served by students seeking their qualifying contracts. From Tuesday through Thursday, the quality moves up a notch, as the students on the two-year course at the Ecole Supérieure de Cuisine Française (ESCF) serve up a €22 menu that, according to their boss, is 'equal to that of a 1-star Michelin restaurant.' Dinner on Thursday evenings for €35.

Soft drinks at the unbeatable price of €1.

LE BAR

27, rue de Condé 75006 Paris
- Access: M° Odéon
- Tel.: 01 43 29 06 61
- Open Mon-Thurs 9.30pm-3am and Fri-Sat 9.30-5am. Closed Sundays

*Keep it
to yourselves...*

If you ask residents in the neighbourhood what lies behind the black window on the corner of rue de Condé and rue Régnault, most of them will tell you that it's a hostess bar with an unsavoury clientele that's best avoided.

Don't believe a word of it. Ring the bell and enter one of the least-known but most pleasant bars in the French capital.

Some even say it's the best bar in the world! Be that as it may, the fact is we've never met anyone who didn't like this secret drinking venue.

Opened in 1982, Le Bar hasn't changed its decor since its origins and that's all to the good. Soft lighting, Asiatic statuettes illuminated by tightly-focused designer spotlights, very cosy leather sofas…

Adding to the appeal, the cocktails are superb (starting at €9).

Ideal for a romantic meeting or a last drink before better things.

CLUB DES POÈTES

30, rue de Bourgogne 75007 Paris
- Access: M° Varenne or Invalides
- Tel.: 01 47 05 06 03
- www.poesie.net
- Open daily, except Saturday lunch time and Sundays.
- Dinner at 8pm, show at 10pm. Dinner menu €20.

Friends of poetry, bonsoir!

The Club des Poètes is one of those rare and precious venues in a city where one enjoys the sensation, for a brief instant, of stepping outside of time. Only a short walk from the National Assembly, Jean-Pierre Rosnay and his wife Marcelle welcome poetry lovers for a drink or dinner. There are even a few foreign enthusiasts who come regularly without speaking a word of French, but nevertheless take delight in the intimate atmosphere and the sonority of the poems declaimed there.

Created in 1961 in order to 'render poetry contagious and inevitable' because it is 'the anti-pollutant of mental space, the counterweight and antidote to an existence that tends to turn us all into robots', the Club des Poètes has received visits from many renowned poets such as Pablo Neruda, Octavio Paz, and Ma Desheng.

The place itself is intriguing: the massive wooden door with its small wrought iron opening, like in the Middle Ages, forcing any latecomers who show up after the poetry sessions have begun to undergo inspection, sets a certain tone. Although you can dine here at a reasonable price (€15 or €20 for a menu), the food, typically French, is not unforgettable although quite decent. The poetry lovers, most of them regulars, arrive one by one. Monsieur Rosnay, junior, son of the founder, who is gradually beginning to take over the reins of the establishment, fusses over his youngest child with his wife, Yasmine… The ambience could not be more familial. Just like in your own home, or almost, there are books scattered about the room and even in the loo. Towards 10pm, Monsieur Rosnay, senior, begins the evening's recitals: classic poems, modern poems, even ones he composed himself. Then there's a brief intermission, to finish dessert, before things start up again. The lights go down, then back on for a moment, and for nearly two hours family members, regulars and more occasional customers take turns in the spotlight, publicly declaiming a poem of their choice. If the diction varies according to the performer, the pleasure of listening is always present, and the atmosphere is wonderful, alternately hushed then enthused. In order to enjoy the experience to the utmost, before coming make the effort to learn a poem and dare yourself to recite it aloud!

Les Carnets
du
Club des Poètes

1

CARNET

Dans le cadre de la manifestation «Ingénieurs et Poètes» et sous le Haut
Patronnage du Ministère de la Culture et de la Communication
l'Ecole Nationale Supérieure de l'Electronique et de ses Applications
et Jean-Pierre Rosnay présentent

Les Illuminations

Spectacle Poésie-Musique

Rimbaud

interprété

par

le Club des
Poètes

Mozart

servi par

le Quatuor

Michel
Deneuve

Maison de Quartier de Cergy Saint-Christophe
Samedi 19 octobre 1991 à 20h30

La journée débutera à 15h par la visite de l'Axe Majeur suivie, à 17h, de la remise des
poésie ENSEA/Club des Poètes et de nouvelle ENSEA/Taille Réelle au Centre Pascal
Batignolles. Et si le cœur vous en dit, nous vous accueillerons, à 19h, aux Rencontres et
sur le thème des liens fructueux entre Science et Poésie qui précèderont le spectacle

Prix des places (nombre limité) : 50F pour le spectacle. 70F
journée (Tarif réduit pour les étudiants et les groupes)
Réservations et renseignements à l'ENSEA-Les Plumes de l'Axe
Le Club des Poètes : 47 05 06 03 ou 3615 code CLP

DEFI Jeunes

BP

BAR-RESTAURANT DE L'AVIATION CLUB DE FRANCE

104, avenue des Champs-Elysées 75008 Paris
• Access: M° Charles-de-Gaulle-Etoile
• Restaurant open daily 8pm-11pm, Mon-Sat 12noon-3pm
• Bar open daily 24hrs. Breakfast 6am-10am
• Menus: €25 and €30

Unchanged since the 50's

Opened to the public in January 2004, the bar-restaurant of the Aviation Club de France is probably the best-kept secret in the entire Champs-Elysées neighbourhood. There's no blinking neon or any other conspicuous sign, simply a menu that sits before the entrance to this club created in 1907.

On the first floor, the reception desk takes down your personal details: this is, after all, still a gambling club, and as everyone knows, one can quickly lose one's head in a card game… After passing through the bar, there are two dining rooms, full of a quiet atmos-

phere that has probably remains unchanged since the 1950s. Once you've been seated you have a choice of two menus priced at €25 and courses €30, or you can pick individual starters à la carte for around €10 and main dishes for about €20. Simple and abundant, the food is rather good if a little rich. You will probably have trouble finishing your dessert with the €30 menu! The bread is top-quality, and the service is attentive and efficient, probably due to the fact that there are still relatively few customers coming here… This is a good adress, offering considerable value for money.

FOYER DE LA MADELEINE

Place de la Madeleine
- Access: M° Madeleine
- Open Mon-Fri, 12noon-1.30pm
- €7 per person for members
- Membership card €2

*Volunteer
feeding force*

A few steps away from the superb Art Nouveau WCs at place de la Madeleine, on the east side of the church, there is a discreet sign that reads 'Foyer de la Madeleine'. Follow the path and go through the gates before descending the small stairway. This will lead you into some splendid cellar vaults dating from the 17th century, beneath the Madeleine church. Hand over, with a smile, €2 for your membership in the association, along with the modest fee of €7, and you're in. Founded by the neighbourhood parish, the Foyer is a Christian association operating according to French legislation passed in 1901. This means that the association's restaurant can only serve members, which explains why you needed to acquire that membership card at the entrance. Only the kitchen staff are salaried employees, while the women waiting tables, usually with great courtesy and speed, are all volunteers. So you see, good service is not always a question of money…

Of course, one doesn't come here for the quality of the cuisine, the chips aren't always as crisp as you might like, and the meat is not necessarily as tender as your heart, but you do eat decently for an extremely low price, especially for this chic neighbourhood. There's a choice of three very simple starters (tomatoes, celery, pâté), one of two main dishes, and either yoghurt or a creamy dessert to finish things off, without being too fussy.

At the end of the vaulted corridor, a second corridor offers seats for those who want to enjoy a quiet coffee. Don't forget to have a look at the paintings of rather dubious taste hanging on the bare stone walls, they are for sale.

LES SALONS DU PARC MONCEAU

8, rue Alfred-de-Vigny 75008 Paris
• Access: M° Courcelles
• Bar-restaurant open daily to the general public 7pm-10pm, except on Tuesdays and Saturdays, which are tournament days when the restaurant is reserved to club members until the start of play (at around 9.15pm-9.30pm)
• Around €20 per person

A magnificent secret terrace

This bridge club tucked away alongside the Monceau park is an exceptional and surprising venue. From the outside, there's absolutely nothing to indicate the presence of a restaurant open to the general public within the walls of this distinguished establishment.

The first glimpse of the inner courtyard is already a delight to the eye: the buildings in the same style as the place des Vosges in brick and stone are absolutely superb. Straight ahead of you, a small stairway leads up to the first floor and the entrance to the club. Upon entering, one finds the bar, behind a first gaming room where one can admire a handsome fireplace. To the right is the main room, and to the right again, another small room used principally by those wishing to dine.

The atmosphere is inimitable. Numerous bridge table occupy an entire smoke-filled room. The players curse or cheer one another on. It's like being in a bridge version of The Color of Money. When ordering a bite to eat in a nook of the dining room, you find yourself feeling the tension that floats in the charged air. The croque-monsieur still goes down nicely, however, accompanied by an agreeable glass of Brouilly.

Obviously, the clientele is neither trendy nor very young. But the time one spends here, almost stolen from eternity, is one of those delicious moments when one reminds oneself how pleasant it is not to have to put on appearances in case an acquaintance happens to pass by.

In summer, this joy of discovery and sense of fulfilment becomes close to miraculous. The doors of the main room are opened up to create a magnificent terrace, looking directly out onto the Monceau park!

Seven to eight tables, adjoining the park, invite you to relax amidst the trees and the singing of the birds, without the sound of car horns. The simplicity of the place and the fact that most Parisians are unaware of its existence makes this paradise accessible at almost any time, even when reserving at the last minute. On very hot days, the proximity of the trees and the park tends to lower the temperature of the terrace by 4-5°C compared to the city streets. Simply exceptional.

L'ATELIER DES CHEFS

10, rue de Penthièvre 75008 Paris
- Access: M° Miromesnil or Franklin-Roosevelt
- Reservation by telephone (01 53 30 05 82)
or by Internet at: www.atelierdeschefs.com
- Closed Sundays
- Lesson + one dish € 15 at lunch time and € 34 evenings (with a 1 hr. lesson)

Other addresses:
- 35, boulevard Haussmann, Lafayette maison (étage -1), 75009 Paris
- 27, rue Péclet, 75015 Paris
- 21, cours de Vincennes, Printemps Nation (étage 4), 75020 Paris

Baking your cake and eating it

Opened in July 2004, the Atelier des Chefs has become a growing success and won't remain a secret for very long! You'd better hurry, therefore, to try out this new concept combining a restaurant with cooking lessons.

The idea is simple: the Bergerault brothers wanted to bring cooking lessons to the masses. To make them accessible to everyone, even those who lack the means to learn the rudiments of French culinary arts at the Ducasse school, they came up with an easy solution: the basic lesson lasts only half an hour and is followed by tasting the dish you have cooked yourself.

Reserve ahead of time and don't be late, because lessons start right on schedule. Put on your plastic apron, set yourself behind your little counter, and you're off. The kindly chef, who wears a superb apron with his name on it (so you'll take him seriously!), passes around the tables, giving out instructions and advice.

Thirty convivial minutes later, you move over to the dining table behind the window. Those of you who choose the first lesson at 12.30pm had better eat quickly because at 1.45 the second lot of students joins the table. Those who want to take their time will thus prefer the lesson that starts at 1.15, or even the evening lesson which lasts a whole hour.

Around the table, in a friendly atmosphere, participants chat with one another - they've already made acquaintance while pouring eggs into the pan - and sometimes discover they share friends in the neighbourhood… The Atelier is in fact only a short distance from the Elysée palace and many banks, consultants, auditors, and lawyers have their offices nearby…

For those who are still hungry after consuming their own dish, there's cheese (an excellent saint-Marcellin was served on the day of our visit) and dessert (a very good tarte aux figues) are available. With a small glass of wine and coffee, the bill comes to around €22-€23 for a pleasant, high-quality meal.

A good address.

CAFÉTÉRIA DU CENTRE COMMUNAUTAIRE JUIF DE PARIS

119, rue Lafayette 75010 Paris
- Access: M° Gare-du-Nord
- Tel.: 01 53 20 52 71
- Open Mon-Thurs 11am-6pm, and Fridays 11am-3pm
- Lunch served until 3pm
- About €12 to €15 per person

A secret terrace in the sunshine

You don't come to 119 rue Lafayette by accident. Home of the Centre Communautaire Juif de Paris, the fifth floor of this building possesses above all a remarkable terrace restaurant looking straight south.

If it isn't really warm outside, the interest of this venue wanes, because inside it does in fact strongly resemble a cafeteria…

But on days when the weather is good, buzz the intercom, climb up to the fifth floor and settle down at one of the least-known terraces in the capital. Don't be surprised if you're greeted with a warm 'shalom', it's perfectly normal. Answer politely and enjoy the view.

To the right there's the Eiffel Tower, to the left buildings from the Haussmann era, and straight in front of you, the sun.

The service is particularly friendly and you can enjoy decent lunch for €9 (salad plus the dish of the day).

LE P'TIT BAR

7, rue Richard Lenoir 75011 Paris
- Access: M° Charonne
- No telephone
- Open daily until around 2am

***A surreal
ambiance***

Le P'tit Bar is one of those rare places that must be savoured with the delicate tenderness a living historic monument deserves. Madame Paolo is a unique character, far removed from current fashions and with no airs and graces whatsoever. Once you enter, you'll immediately understand why we urge you to come and have a drink here, just to be able to say one day, "I, too, spent some time in Madame Paulo's P'tit Bar".

The indescribable atmosphere that reigns here is a mixture of calm, torpor, and a journey into the past certain to appeal to the nostalgic.

One of the few reproaches that can be made about the place is the lack of cleanliness, to put things mildly. If you arrive at the right moment, behind the front door you'll see Madame Paulo feeding her birds and caressing them affectionately, heedless of the birdseed spilling all around… Similarly, if you find yourself looking nervously at the stains on your glass after a trip to the toilet, and losing touch with the magic of the moment due to worries about hygiene, you'd best stay away. The last time we paid a visit, there was a sponge so mouldy that we wondered what the landlady had been using it for…

But the customers make up for this. If you're feeling a little lonely, this place may very well cheer you up. It's not particularly lively, but no matter how many people are there (on a good evening, four or five – note that there's only room for about a dozen), you can be sure of chatting to one of them, or at worst (best?) with Madame Paulo herself.

It's not for everyone. Don't come here if you're going to make fun of Madame Paulo's age or her outmoded way of expressing herself. The customers are sometimes totally surreal…   just like the place itself.

RESTAURANT ITINÉRANT D'ART CONTEMPORAIN

Contact : Art Process, 52, rue Sedaine 75011 Paris
- Tel.: 01 47 00 90 85. www.art-process.com
- E-mail: infof@art-process.com
- Dinner every fourth Tuesday of the month
- €50 per person

A contemporary moveable art feast

Organized by the Art Process gallery, these itinerant contemporary art dinners will delight both lovers of modern art and culinary inventiveness. Held the fourth Tuesday of every month, each time in a different venue, these dinners are an original and appealing way of keeping abreast of contemporary art.

The day we went, the dinner took place at Anne de Villepoix's gallery in rue de Montmorency, which presented several canvasses by a Chinese artist.

Having been relieved of a €50 bill at the door, first of all you get a little introductory speech outlining the evening's theme. That evening, forty guests listened to two or three speakers on the theme of private collections, moderated by Eric Mezan, the head of Art Process. With a cocktail created by a 'culinary designer' in your hand, you lend a somewhat distracted ear to the commentary while watching the other guests with interest. Rather homogeneous and drawn mainly from the art world, the audience appears to be friendly. After a guided tour of the gallery, it's time for dinner, seated on a sheet around a thermos of tea and several large bottles of (good) saké. The people mix in an easy fashion and conversations get started. Not for very long, unfortunately, because the dinner is devoted above all to the planned debates, which everyone is supposed to listen to attentively.

The debates are not all that interesting, in any case, and take place in an atmosphere that to an outsider may seem a trifle self-indulgent and pretentious. You find yourself wishing several times that things could be a little less formal, notably in the way the debates proceed. The food, very 'design', offers small but rather good and always inventive mouthfuls, served parsimoniously by a waiter dressed completely in black with a severe demeanour. The meal leaves you feeling a little hungry - there's a long wait until (a very nice) dessert allows you go home more or less replete.

The best moments, looking back, are before, and above all, after dinner, when the saké begins to have its effect and make people talkative. Conversation grows animated and contacts are made. As the evening comes to a close, you see people exchanging e-mail addresses and telephone numbers, with promises to send invitations to a future trendy vernissage or a forthcoming performance by a young Korean artist.

LA CIPALE

51, avenue de Gravelle 75012 Paris
• Access: M° Liberté or Charenton-Ecoles
• Tel.: 01 43 75 54 53
• www.restaurant.la-cipale.com
• Open noon and evenings, Mon-Fri
• Menu €32

A meal at the Velodrome

Located within the city limits of Paris, but only thanks to the appendage of Vincennes park which allows the French capital to improve its official statistics concerning open spaces, La Cipale is a little-known but appealing restaurant that is geographically much closer to the suburb of Charenton. So we don't advise you to try walking there from Paris!

If you get off at the Charenton-Ecoles Métro station, don't stop at the La Cipale restaurant on the avenue Jean-Jaurès, it isn't the right one. Keep on going until you reach the edge of Vincennes park, where you'll see the entrance to the Jacques-Anquetil velodrome. It's in there.

Occupying the former house of the velodrome's porter, the restaurant has a very beautiful terrace, completely isolated from any automobile traffic. In winter, the fireplace and the handsome interior decoration which preserves some mementoes from the glory days of the velodrome, create a warm atmosphere.

The nearby presence of the historic cycling circuit, where races are still held, and the rundown cyclists' sheds on either side of the restaurant also lend this venue a quaint, almost anachronistic aura that is quite pleasant.

The cuisine however, is very much up-to-date. There's a very lively menu priced at €32 (starter-main course-dessert), along with some well-presented speciality dishes including a very successful risotto de Saint-Jacques and an enjoyable pastilla de figues.

After your meal, go for a walk around the velodrome stands. With a little luck, you will see some cyclists doing a few laps on the track. There's an entrance just to the right, behind the restaurant. Built in 1894, the La Cipale velodrome, as it was originally named, occupies a special place in French sporting history. Shortly after its construction, it hosted many events in the Olympic Games of 1900, notably cricket, rugby, and football matches. For that occasion, it was enlarged by the addition of two lateral stands. But above all, La Cipale remains enshrined in the hearts of the numerous lovers of the petite reine ('little queen', the French nickname for the bicycle). Having been the scene of the final stage of many past Tours de France, La Cipale was also where French cycling idol Jacques Anquetil bid farewell to his Parisian fans in 1969.

BANGKOK THAÏLANDE

35, boulevard Auguste-Blanqui 75013 Paris
- Access: M° Corvisart or Place-d'Italie
- Tel.: 01 45 80 76 59
- Open daily, except Sundays and Mondays lunch time

*Thai
seduction*

It starts as soon as you reserve a table. You give your name and an extremely friendly voice answers you using your first name, 'Of course, monsieur Jacques, see you soon, monsieur Jacques…' When you arrive, the same mode of address continues, as if they've known you your entire life. Could be a little tricky if you've just told your dining companion that it's the first time you've ever been there…

As you sit at your table, monsieur Kam whispers in your ear, but loudly enough so your partner can hear, that it's an excellent table for kissing. Then, after calling you 'the lovebirds', he leaves you for a moment. The scene has been set and now nothing will stop it from running on.

When it comes time to order, the play continues. Monsieur Kam recommends the spicy beef, adding, 'It's good for your energy,' with a sly wink.

A resident of France for over 35 years now, our friend knows a good deal about such matters: in addition to his official wife in Paris, he has three others in Thailand that he returns to see regularly.

With decent food at a very reasonable price, a welcome that encourages sensuality, and a charming decor, you'll have a very good time. Go there, with the appropriate partner.

MAISON PERSONNELLE DE JIM HAYNES

75014 Paris
• Access: M° Alésia
• E-mail: jim.haynes@wanadoo.fr
• €20 per person

Jim'll fix it

For over 25 years now, Jim Haynes, a young American in his sixties, has been inviting strangers into his home. Every Sunday evening, except in summer, he receives guests in his very beautiful artist's studio in the 14th arrondissement, some of whom he does not know at all, and others only slightly, because they've been there before

Varying between 40 in winter and 80 to 90 in warm days - spilling out merrily onto the cobbled private alleyway that adjoins his studio -, people come to these Sunday events to mingle joyfully and politely chat one another up.

An international crowd, made up largely of Americans passing through - Jim has been the subject of an article in the United Airlines flight magazine -, English expatriates and curious, open-minded French natives, bumps shoulders, glass of wine in hand, in an easy-going atmosphere.

For newcomers, it all begins via Internet: send Jim an e-mail at the address given above and wait for the reply. If the maximum capacity of his home hasn't yet been reached - this happens sometimes and Jim then has to draw up waiting lists! - he'll get back to you quickly, giving you his phone number and asking you to call him on the appointed day to find out his address and access code.

The actual arrival is surprising. The green gate, as promised, conceals a beautiful private alleyway leading to several artists' studios tucked away in the greenery. It's charming. The hubbub of voices provides an easy beacon, and using your elbows, you make your way up to Jim in person, who immediately begins introducing everyone to everyone. Thanks to his stupendous memory, Jim remembers the first names of practically all the guests! 'Jacques, this is Jenny, Jenny this is Jacques, Thomas here is Marleen, Steve, Peter, Nicole, Françoise.' You are thus rapidly brought into the picture and immediately start to talk with this friendly guy named Peter who you don't know from Adam, but that's the whole spirit of the thing. Usually about fifty years old, your typical guest is single, a teacher, an artist, or a lawyer, and beyond the pleasures of conversation, is visibly ready for more if the feeling is mutual.

Before leaving, don't forget to give Jim your contribution in an envelope with your name on it. €20 per head, that seems reasonable and it allows Jim to honour the motto posted on one of his walls: 'Jim's plan: stay home and get paid.'

CAFÉ-RESTAURANT AUTO PASSION

197, boulevard Brune 75014 Paris
• Access: M° Porte-d'Orléans
• Tel.: 01 45 43 20 20
• Open daily 9.30am-2am (Sundays: 4pm-2am)
• About €25 per person

Have a drink on a Formula 1 engine

Before you even go into the bar, the tone is set. On the pavement outside, a shiny petrol pump has been diverted from its primary function and displays the menu. The front door handles are aluminium wheel rims, the armchairs are bucket seats, and the beer pumps are cylinders of Castrol oil with gear boxes attached. For those of you who really get into details, even some of the lamps have been made out of extra-large exhaust pipes from racing cars! Once you've recovered from the initial shock, you sit down quietly and set your drink on a transparent table that showcases a turbo engine.

Who hasn't dreamt of having a drink over a Formula 1 engine?

Other engines of all different types are scattered about the room, including one that's ensured for €500,000. 'One never knows,' the owner says quite seriously. 'One day a guy may try to hold up the bar just to steal that engine…'

After you've drunk your beer and glanced through one of the numerous specialized magazines available, make your way to the loo, which is the jewel in the crown of this mad decor.

Taking a few seconds to acclimatize yourself - you've just passed by numerous objects, letters, and other documents on display throughout the entire bar -, gather your wits and try not to choke. The hand drier is in fact a Formula 1 racing helmet. You'll come back to that. Go into one of the cabins, sit down and belt up, just like in a racing car, for what may be a rough ride… The toilet paper is dispensed from another wheel rim.

Truly astonishing. And the food's good, too.

LE CAFÉ DES SPORTS - CHEZ YANEK WALCZAK

75, rue Brancion 75015 Paris
• Access: M° Porte-de-Vanves
• Tel.: 01 48 28 61 00
• Lunch menu € 16

*La Belle
Équipe*

The first time one goes to Yanek Walczak's venue is always a bit of a surprise. Standing before 75 rue Brancion, you are first of all astonished by the front of the establishment. No sign of any lights on inside. There's not even a doorknob. By all appearances, the place is closed and your friend has given you a bad tip. But putting your trust in a friendship that's lasted over twenty years, you remain patient and then suddenly it occurs to you to raise your head and peek over the top of the lace curtain. And there, quietly sitting at tables in the shadows, you see people are having lunch. You knock at the door, which miraculously opens for you, and Yanek even shakes your hand warmly. So, you're in. Because the right to eat at the Café des Sports has to be earned. Yanek Walczak, the owner, only likes to serve people he knows (friends or regular customers, often one and the same) or those he has a good feeling about. And therefore, by virtue of a concept that might even seem extremely avant-garde, he deliberately tries to give the odd passing tourist or visitor to the nearby Georges-Brassens park the impression that the restaurant isn't actually open.

Evidently, the idea works, and roundabout 1pm, the dining room, plunged into darkness so absolutely nothing can be detected from outside, is full.

The atmosphere is straight out of one of Audiard's films and one expects Jean Gabin to emerge at any moment from the back room. A photo of Brassens highlights the boss's acquaintances from the past. Other, more numerous photos recall his career as a boxer. His father even once had a bout with the great Marcel Cerdan. The customers shout out to one another, and also shout to you. The very good wine is drunk straight from the (magnum) bottles. The starters are laid out on a tray in front of you. There are generous portions of terrine and whole sausages. You help yourself, just like at home. 'After all, let's not pretend like we're in a restaurant,' says the owner, mockingly. Other customers knock on the front door window and sit down next to you. Bottles of wine are exchanged. You sample your neighbour's white wine, and pass him the rillettes.

If the cuisine isn't exactly light on the stomach, it is good and abundant. And with a menu priced at €16, who would complain about spending time in the presence of such atmospheric mugs?

VILLA TOSCANE

36-38, rue des Volontaires 75015 Paris
• Access: M° Volontaires
• Tel.: 01 43 06 82 92
• Closed Saturday lunch time and Sundays
• Menu €27

Hidden away on a quiet street in the 15th arrondissement, Villa Toscane is a small marvel of a romantic restaurant. Offering adorable hospitality, excellent Italian food at reasonable prices, and a warm, romantic ambience, what more can you wish for?

Discreet and romantic

All the more so because it's not yet very well-known and you may regularly find yourselves the only diners in the place. Which allows you plenty of time to chat about Italy with the charming owner.

Seated at your table illuminated by a small candle, one takes pleasure in examining the assortment of decorative elements: authentic Venetian mirrors, numerous chandeliers, but only four tables in the main dining room, with

eventually another one on the opposite side of the entrance…
One almost has the impression of not being in a restaurant.
For those who may feel sleepy from the Tuscan wine, the Villa Toscane also has some small but cosy rooms above, for €90 and €100 per night.
The very fine menu with starter-main course-dessert is €27, or €23 if you skip either the starter or dessert. Above all, try the superb *jambon de Parme*, the *raviolis aux artichauts*, the *pâtes aux aubergines*, as well as the delicious zabaïone for dessert.

OM'ZAKI

76, rue de la Procession 75015 Paris
- Access: M° Pernety or Plaisance
- Tel.: 01 56 58 08 82
- Open daily, except Saturday lunch time and Sundays
- Menus from € 12.50

A Palestinian village restaurant

Looking in from the street, you get the impression that the friend who gave you this address may have been pulling your leg. It seems like a very ordinary dining venue similar to most of Lebanese restaurants you already know. Except for the fact that Om'zaki is not Lebanese, but Syro-Palestinian. And once you pass through the first dining room, you are enchanted to discover the marvellous inner courtyard that lies hidden among the various buildings.

Surrounded by walls painted in blue and white, this little patio has an exotic, disorienting quality that's very pleasant. You almost feel like you're in either the backyard of a small Greek village or at some country home in the Middle East. On sunny days, the seven or eight tables outside are protected by an arbour from which very real bunches of grapes burst forth.

The food, which is quite correct, is priced at around €5 for starters and desserts, and €12 to €15 for main courses. A copious plate of assorted starters costs €10, with a lunch menu for €12.50 and an evening menu for €20.50. There's

wine available from €18 to €22 per bottle. The service is charming, very much in the tradition of Middle Eastern hospitality. For the price of a single mint tea, your glass is refilled indefinitely, just as Inès's daughter does for her grandmother, who lives in the small house at the top of the stairs on the far side of the patio…

KAISEKI SUSHI

Rue André-Lefèvre 75015 Paris
- Access: M° Javel
- www.kaiseki.com
- Reservation only, call: 01 45 54 48 60
- Around €50 per person

"

A secret Japanese master of gastronomy

Kaiseki Sushi is probably one of the most amazing restaurants in the French capital. This story begins in a soulless street, between various new buildings in a rapidly transforming Javel neighbourhood next to the Citroën park. So, make sure you have one that's completely up-to-date, before going up this particular street. On the right, nothing. On the left, nothing either, not a trace of a restaurant. The street being quite short, you start back down again in the opposite direction. Still nothing. That's normal, because there really is no indication on the outside. And only Japanese-speakers who can decipher kanji, the Chinese characters employed in the Japanese language, will be able to read the inscription hidden behind the restaurant's window.

So, when you see some Asiatic characters behind a window, tell yourself that you've found the right place, and push through the door. Half of the tiny room is occupied by the open kitchen, what Hisayuki Takeuchi calls his 'laboratory of new Japanese cuisine.' The other half of the room features a large rectangular dining table where everyone squeezes in, elbow to elbow. The space by the door is the best place to have a Japanese beer while observing the extraordinary dexterity of the chef as he prepares your order.

The menu is simple, there is none. 'How many are you, now?' Hisa asks you. 'Three? Very good!' And he starts to prepare, without asking you anything further, sushis, sashimis cut straight from the fresh fish delivered that morning from the Rungis wholesale market by an expert Japanese buyer, makis, and other succulent Japanese fare, some familiar and others less so.

The quality of the cuisine is quite exceptional, and we will probably not be alone in proclaiming Kaiseki Sushi one of the best Japanese restaurants in Paris. All of it served with extreme simplicity, from the straightforward but cordial hospitality to a decor that's barely better than that of some institutional canteen.It comes as no surprise that the Japanese embassy calls on his services for official ceremonies.

The only welcome decorative touch in this somewhat stark setting are the immense plates of 19th century Japanese porcelain, collected by his grandfather in Japan, which Hisa uses for his preparations. An absolute must.

BAR-RESTAURANT DU GOLF DU BOIS DE BOULOGNE

Hippodrome d'Auteuil, 75016 Paris
- Access : M° Porte-Auteuil
- Tel.: 01 44 30 70 00
- www.golfduboisdeboulogne.fr - E-mail : sgb@wanadoo.fr

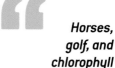

Horses, golf, and chlorophyll

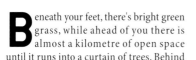

Beneath your feet, there's bright green grass, while ahead of you there is almost a kilometre of open space until it runs into a curtain of trees. Behind you, the same. To the sides, the lawn also stretches a great distance before ending at a line of trees. Not a single automobile can be heard. Your neighbour gravely orders a 'chose' from the waiter who without batting an eyelid goes off to the kitchen to fetch it.

This miracle of an open-air restaurant is located right in the middle of the Auteuil racetrack. For several years now, as soon as the horses get a rest, golfers invade the central area of the track. There's a putting green, two practice zones, and an approach zone for the short game. Except for an actual course, all the elements of the sport are here.

For non-golfers, however, the most interesting feature is the bar-restaurant by the practice zones, which has an exceptional location along the boulevard des Maréchaux. With chlorophyll, sunshine when weather permits, and pretty girls (possibly attracted by the deep pockets of our golfer friends?), the spot is almost perfect.

Unfortunately, except for the dream location, the rest is really not up to scratch: the service is old-fashioned and very slow, and the quality of the food is mediocre. But you didn't come here for that, so make do with a drink.

A 'chose', for example, the golfing drink par excellence, a mixture of grapefruit juice and Schweppes which effectively quenches the golfers' thirst when they return from the course or the practice zone.

Another star drink here is the chantaco: 1/4 orange juice, 1/4 grapefruit juice, 1/4 lemon juice, and 1/4 strawberry syrup.

Before coming, don't forget to call and make sure no horse races are taking place. Otherwise, you risk finding yourself caught up in a different kind of scene…

LE TRINQUET

8, quai Saint-Exupéry 75016 Paris
• Access: M° Exelmans or Porte-de-Saint-Cloud
• Tel.: 01 40 50 09 25
• Open daily for lunch and dinner except Sunday evenings
• Dish of the day € 12

Pelote while you eat

Stuck in an unlikely corner of the 16th arrondissement, a sort of no man's land lying between the Seine riverbank and the Périphérique motorway, you won't come across the Trinquet by accident. From the pavement, there's nothing to indicate the existence of this astonishing little restaurant. So once you locate 8 quai Saint-Exupéry, don't hesitate to enter what looks like a sports stadium. In fact, you're at the Chiquito de Cambo fronton (pelote courts), named after an illustrious player of Basque pelote who died in 1950. A bas-relief of this sporting hero greets you in the entrance.

Continue to your left alongside the court facing the entrance and go into the roofed building that lies just beyond. This houses a trinquet, a particular type of pelote court and the only one of its kind in Paris. Don't be put off by the first room you come to, which is not very exciting.

Separated from the trinquet by a large picture window, the bar-restaurant has not received much media attention. But surrounded by a very provincial atmosphere, where Paris has already become distant, you can sample some simple but good Basque cuisine, while watching players compete in a pelote match through the window.

With a very good Basque pâté for €4.50, a superb osso-buco for €12 and a huge portion of ribs for two costing €28, you certainly get your money's worth here. And for the same price, above all, you get a trip through time and space. If you're feeling really adventurous, it's possible to rent the court for €28 an hour. The management will kindly lend you rackets and ball, leaving you to master the game.

SALON DE THÉ DE MADEMOISELLE LI

Jardin d'Acclimatation
• Bois de Boulogne 75016 Paris
• Access : métro Les Sablons
• Open Saturdays and Sundays 12noon-6pm

Mademoiselle Li's tea-room is a rare and precious venue that must be savoured slowly, like the Chinese tea that is served there.

First of all, pay the €2.50 fee at the main entrance to the Jardin d'Acclimatation, which you won't regret.

A rare and precious venue that must be savoured slowly

Located in a former warehouse with a surface of 350 m2, the tea-room is decorated with antique Chinese furniture, traditional lanterns, wooden and lacquered panels, and obviously some tables and chairs.

There are very few customers on this spring Saturday, the weather is fine, people are outdoors, and it's usually on Sundays that the tea-room is busiest. It's an ideal opportunity to become acquainted Hippolyte Romain, artistic director of the Jardin d'Acclimatation and founder, ten years ago, of this magical, timeless establishment.

About sixty years old, Hippolyte is quite a character. If you strike the right note and he takes a liking to you, he'll willingly abandon the painting he's working on to tell you a multitude of fascinating stories about China, Venice, Rome, or his life in general. A life that has been richly filled, after having spent some time in the fashion scene. He frequently visits Beijing, where he owns an old house, and Venice, which he adores. Get him to talk, you won't regret it. He may even show you some of the furniture he has gathered here, such as an amazing double chest into which Chinese merchants would place the money from their sales before sleeping in it at night in order to discourage bandits. Or a very beautiful 17th century chest for storing rugs made from camphor wood in order to drive off moths and other insects.

His young red-headed companion, Jeanne, serves tea with grace and delicacy. €4 for a pot of very good Chinese tea expertly selected by Hippolyte, but the price matters little. Hippolyte is not seeking to make money. He's trying above all to share his joy in being here and offering himself the luxury of spending whatever time he likes talking to those willing to accept this gift.

Yellow tea, red tea, trust him, he'll know how to chose the right one for the occasion. Don't hesitate either to come spend a quiet moment on your own here. There are lots of books just waiting to be read or merely glanced at. Or else you can simply remain silent and still for a long moment to soak up the atmosphere of the place and meditate on the example of a man who has visibly succeeded in living out his dream.

CAFÉ-RESTAURANT DU PALAIS DE CHAILLOT

Place du Trocadéro 75016 Paris
- Access : métro Trocadéro
- Open before performances on theatre nights
- Dinner: about €25 per person

*Dinner
and theatre
by the Eiffel Tower*

Instructions: find out in Pariscope or other Paris listings which evenings shows are playing at the palais de Chaillot. These frequently start at around 8.30pm. Arrive at place du Trocadéro by 7pm. The palais de Chaillot is the building on the left looking from the square. To the right an impressive stairway in Art Deco style, like the entire Trocadéro complex built in the 1930s, extends its arms to you.

Don't be intimidated and go down the stairs with a confident air. You don't require a ticket yet. At the far end to the right, a big room looks out over the Trocadéro esplanade. Still no need of a ticket. Before you, majestic, rises the Eiffel Tower. You sit down at one of the tables, with a Martini on the rocks. You're in just the right spot. A few minutes later, the Eiffel Tower begins to sparkle madly. Your companion looks at you longingly and places a languorous arm around your neck.

There are two solutions here: either go back upstairs and purchase two tickets for the theatre play that starts in 20 minutes, or return home to celebrate this magic moment stolen from the real theatregoers.

But a very decent dinner is also possible. You have the right to finish your meal even after the curtain rises.

LE BISTRO DES DAMES - L'ELDORADO

18, rue des Dames 75017 Paris
- Access: M° Place-de-Clichy
- Tel.: 01 45 22 13 42
- No reservations
- Open daily
- Around €25 per person

A superb hidden garden

Although it's totally undetectable from the street, the Bistro des Dames has probably one of the most pleasant terraces in Paris. There are two ways of gaining access to it, either by passing straight through the bistro, or by entering the Hôtel Eldorado, whose very pleasant and reasonably priced rooms also overlook this sublime courtyard-garden.

Entry by the hotel is preferable because it's more surprising. Just go down the small hallway and you'll find it. Ten tables accommodate those lucky

enough to know about this superb address, which is obviously more worthwhile visiting in the summer. It's just too bad that warm weather isn't more frequent in the French capital…

The food is simple, correct, and French. Expect to end up paying €20-€30 per person.

Just one slight quibble: the service is sadly rather irregular, and you sometimes encounter waiters who border on discourtesy. It's a pity they haven't absorbed a little more of the serenity that dwells in this particular spot.

WAGON BLEU

7, rue Boursault 75017 Paris
• Access: M° Rome
• Tel.: 01 45 22 35 25. Fax: 01 45 22 35 64
• Open 12noon-2am except Sundays
• Around €20 to €25 per person

**Dine
in a wagon from
the legendary
Orient Express**

Built in 1927, one of the wagons from the legendary Orient-Express train linking Paris to Venice and the East finished its wandering years in the Gare Saint-Lazare. In 1958, it found itself being lifted by a giant crane from the rails on which it had always rested, only to be deposited on the pavement adjacent to the huge sunken trough formed by the railways as they enter this Parisian terminus.

After changing owners several times, the wagon has now been converted into a bar-restaurant. The internal decor of the wagon has remained practically intact: the original velvet upholstery is still there, as are the baggage racks. Two suitcases pretend they are waiting for a passenger to arrive at his or her destination.

There's an uninterrupted view of the suburban trains wending their way between Paris and Viroflay, Asnières, La Défense, Bécon-les-Bruyères... Far less exotic than Constantinople, but you can almost believe that you're bound for the latter, especially in the evening, with the help of small candles that provide some semblance of a romantic atmosphere. The cuisine is simple but good.

POLONIA

20, rue Legendre 75017 Paris
- Access: M° Malesherbes, Villiers or Monceau
- Tel.: 01 43 80 10 06
- E-mail : restaurantpolonia@hotmail.com
- Open Tues-Sat, lunch time and evenings
- Around €20 per person

A restaurant with a surprise upstairs

The Polish husband mans the kitchen, while the wife, a Frenchwoman, takes care of the dining room. The Polonia restaurant is a condensed version of Poland itself, somewhat removed from time and fashion. The decor is a little chic, but in an East European manner which inevitably calls to mind those restaurants dating from the Communist era, with their large but somewhat empty dining spaces, trying hard to take on bourgeois airs but indelibly marked by the years behind the Iron Curtain.

For those who want to journey to another time and place, indulge yourself with a delicious *bortsch 'ukrainien'* for €6. This beet soup will appease even those of you who have hated this vegetable ever since the school canteen. The main courses are priced €10-€12. Try the Polish raviolis with meat stuffing and the potato pancakes, also typically Polish (€10).

Those of you who feel a trifle heavy by the end of the meal - despite the quality - should be aware that this restaurant offers you an unexpected opportunity for a short digestive expedition.

On the fourth floor of the town house in which the establishment is located, the Polish association Concorde that manages the place completed restoration in May 2003 of a sublime library that your hosts of the day will be happy to let you discover. The lift is broken and the stairs are steep, but you won't regret it. Perfectly restored, this chamber, which in the past once housed a chapel, was later occupied by a Masonic lodge. Today, the superb neogothic decor remains: wood panelling, paintings, painted caisson ceilings, and a remarkable fireplace. In one corner, a piano waits to be caressed. The room can be rented out for a fee of €500, and would provide an excellent setting for a small concert, a declaration of love by candlelight, or even an elegant dinner among friends. Some cold dishes can be brought up from restaurant's kitchen downstairs.

RESTAURANT chez LUCETTE

le bourgeois
gentilhomme

THEATRE DE LA PORTE ST-MARTIN

chèque
déjeuner

TR

CHEZ LUCETTE

43, rue de La Jonquière 75017 Paris
- Access: M° Guy-Môquet
- Tel./Fax : 01 46 27 72 54
- Open daily lunch time and evenings, except Sunday and Tuesday
- Around €15-€20 per person

The provincial touch

Chez Lucette is a restaurant unaffected by time or passing fashions where one feels strangely at ease.
Although known principally to neighbourhood residents, Lucette does draw in a few gourmands who appreciate in particular the tranquility and conviviality she provides. Located between the boulevard des Maréchaux and Guy-Môquet, there's not really much to visit in the area.

Concealed by lace curtains that give it a very provincial atmosphere, the restaurant makes itself discreet. And as Lucette says, 'Here we don't sell hot air and we don't like publicity.'

An interesting woman, Lucette. Originally from Normandy, as attested to by the succulent crêpes Suzette that she prepares for dessert (€4) or her escalopes à la crème (€8), she alternates with touching sincerity between hot and cold, funny and surprising.

She's cold when you first walk in the door and she studies you in order to make up her mind whether she really wants to accept you in her place. But she grows warmer after the last customers leave, opening up a bit to reveal a certain edgy sensitivity.

She's funny when she recounts with considerable verve the day she saw a guy in the street removing a cold storage cabinet, her cold storage cabinet! And how it was all the result of her flat across the street being squatted by a really cheeky couple who went so far as forging a rental contract which they showed to the police when asked to leave!

She's surprising when you leave a potato on your plate and she scolds you, just like a mother would scold her son for not finishing a meal lovingly prepared for him.

But as far as cooking is concerned, she's good. Very good, in fact, and for prices that are old-fashioned. Just like the decor in her place. Since 1900, almost nothing has changed: the bar, whose age is indicated by the quaint installation for hoisting stock from the storeroom in the cellar, the furniture, and the walls. Only the famous cold storage cabinet has disappeared.

And there's been one addition, a television set in a corner, which Lucette sometimes turns on as a reminder that here we're not in Paris.

INSTITUT VATEL

122, rue Nollet 75017 Paris
- Access: M° Brochant
- Tel.: 01 42 26 26 60
- www.vatel.fr
- Open Mon-Fri lunch time and evenings
- Menus (both lunch and dinner): €26, €30, €33

> *Gastronomes in short pants*

You don't stumble across Vatel by chance: although sign reading 'Institut Vatel' is easily spotted on the street, you'd have to be extraordinarily perspicacious to guess that there was a gastronomic restaurant hiding behind the façade. A school of hotel & restaurant management, the Vatel institute has opted to alternate between theoretical and practical training of its students. Depending on the year of the course they are in, each student thus goes from the classroom to the kitchen or dining room.

The result is surprising: in a chic and contemporary setting (with very beautiful and original luminous panels instead of paintings or prints on the walls), the somewhat stilted reception might be almost intimidating. But very quickly, the appealing amateurism of the waiters has a relaxing effect. You catch yourself smiling at the little errors on the part of the trainees and it becomes a game to observe certain ones, visibly ill at ease (especially at the beginning of the school year, in October-November) commit blunders. On the whole the service, almost excessive numerically (no less than ten students for as many tables), is excellent, or at any rate, trying hard to do things right. All this goes on under the watchful, but occasionally amused eye of the maître d'hôtel-instructor. The cuisine is of a very high standard and the menu at €26 would cost at least twice as much in any classic restaurant. The desserts trolley is particularly impressive: you have the right to sample all of the fifteen desserts available each day.

A very good address offering almost matchless value for your money.

VATEL, THE COOK FOR PRINCE DE CONDÉ

The institute derives its name from François Vatel, who was the cook for Louis II de Bourbon, Prince de Condé, at the château de Chantilly in the 17th century. The film Vatel, starring Gérard Depardieu, relates the reasons why this cook lives on in history: caught short by the announcement of an impending visit by the French monarch Louis XIV to see his mentor, the Grand Condé, and with barely fifteen days to prepare for this momentous occasion, Vatel was faced with the task of feeding nearly 600 courtiers and a total of several thousand other people, domestic servants included, over the course of three days. Unfortunately, a few roasts were missing at some tables during the first dinner. The following morning, the further delay of the so-called 'marée' (tide) or delivery of fresh fish and seafood from Boulogne-sur-Mer finally dishonoured him completely. He went up to his chamber and stabbed himself three times with his sword.

CHEZ ARSÈNE

12, rue Doudeauville 75018 Paris
- Access: M° Marx-Dormoy or Marcadet-Poissonnière
- Tel.: 01 46 07 46 32
- Open almost every weekend until late at night
- Around €15-€20 per person

A refuge in the night

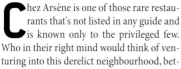hez Arsène is one of those rare restaurants that's not listed in any guide and is known only to the privileged few. Who in their right mind would think of venturing into this derelict neighbourhood, between Marx-Dormoy and the Goutte d'Or ? On foot, not many people, especially at night. So come by car, and park it as close to the address as possible, one always finds spaces. In any event, the police don't come often here to tow away illegally parked vehicles….

Don't be fooled by the ancient front window where you can still read the inscription, 'A la ville de Mâcon.' This is the right place.

Accompanied by a little jazzy music in the background, some soft lights create a romantic ambiance. Some ceramic plates are displayed on the dressed stone walls, most likely vestiges of the restaurant from the period when the owner was still somebody from Mâcon…

Leaning on the bar, Arsène, majestically calm, unruffled, and full of solicitude, is taking care of the few customers present.

'Do you have anything left to eat?' In his accented French, Arsène lets you know in an even tone that if you'd like to eat kid, that would be perfect. Let's try the kid, then. For €8, the risk is small.

Unless you're really hungry: if it happens that the dish does not agree with you, you'll really have to wait a long time for Arsène to prepare another. He takes care of everything on his own: reception, cooking, service, and the bill.

Fortunately, sometimes a customer who has become a friend helps him find glasses, and the bottle of wine…

Transported by the strange atmosphere of the venue and the kindness of the owner, you wouldn't dream of complaining. On the contrary, little by little you find yourself deriving immense pleasure from the lazy tranquillity and the somnolence that has gradually taken hold of you.

BAR LA PETITE RENAISSANCE

36, boulevard d'Ornano 75018 Paris
• Access: M° Simplon
• Open daily 5.30am-2am

The case of the missing ceramics

The Petite Renaissance probably owes its lack of fame to its unglamorous location very close to the porte de Clignancourt. So much the better for local regulars who alone enjoy its many charms. Built in 1893, this small bar takes pride in a magnificent piece of ceramic entitled 'le roi boit' (the king drinks), as well as its friezes dating from the same period, a superb stained-glass window, and an ancient barometer which unfortunately is no longer in working order.

Run in a masterful fashion by Samia and her mother, originally from Algeria, the bar was listed almost by miracle as a protected historic building in 1989. A

US citizen who had bought the ceiling and doors, also composed from ceramic tiles and stained-glass, was arrested by customs in possession of this precious merchandise which he was bringing back home with him. The customs officials who investigated the case were dismayed to learn they could not prevent the sale: the bar was not listed and therefore the transaction was entirely legal. Paradoxically this situation led to the rest of the bar becoming protected.

Be prepared, the majority of customers present are at times overwhelmingly masculine and this may be slightly off-putting for women on their own.

LE NANT

58, rue du Ruisseau 75018 Paris
• Access: M° Jules-Joffrin
• Tel.: 01 46 06 44 75
• Open daily 12noon-2am, except Thursdays

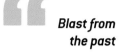

Blast from the past

A truly unlikely café, of which all too few remain in Paris. It has Seventies decorations, but these are the real thing, meaning they actually date back to the Seventies, as opposed to those found in more recent trendy cafés.

The decor is made up of odds and ends: an electric peacock that fans its tail, a photo of Mount Kailas in Tibet offered by a travelling customer, an alcove filled with furniture, and an aging Grundig television set by the entrance. At the rear, more discarded items are stored, with chairs piled up behind a picture puzzle of an Alpine landscape…It's there that Raymond, the bar's owner for the last fifteen years, goes to try to find a little cake to accompany your coffee. Surrounded by replicas of owls in all different sizes displayed behind the counter, Raymond once possessed a live one in his previous bar in the 13th arrondissement. He takes pleasure in showing you

the photo. It's in memory of it that customers have given him all these copies on show…

Sit down on one of the orange Skai bench seats, adjust the lighting with your individual dimmer, and don't bother messing around with the mini juke-box at each table, they haven't worked for a long time now.

The crowd here is mostly old alcoholics and some younger people doing their best to catch up. But it's an experience that takes you back to the past. Be warned, however, the ambience generating from the barflies drawn by the drinks prices which are still set at the same level as in the good old days may be a turn-off for some of our female readers.

PIERRE CARRÉ

LES NOCTAMBULES

24, boulevard de Clichy 75018 Paris
• Access: M° Pigalle
• Tel.: 01 46 06 16 38
• Open daily 5pm-5am, except Sundays, but Pierre Carré is only present
on Thurdays, Fridays and Saturdays, 10.30pm-5am

A true monument of Parisian night-life, Pierre Carré is THE star of Pigalle. At the age of 70 or 80, nobody knows for sure, squeezed into his unreal red suit, with an oiled quiff like that of Lucien (the famous rocker character of French bande-dessinée) in his

Usual suspects

better days, he belts out the old songs from the heydays of Montmartre with a sly sense of humour that can never go out of fashion.

Don't be put off by the banal appearance of the front entrance, it's all happening in the back room under the timeless glints of the inevitable mirrorball. There's a wonderfully mixed, shady crowd of the usual suspects, made up of regulars, elderly nostalgic fans, a few stray tourists, and residents of the neighbourhood. You frequently have strange encounters there that will bring a smile to your lips when you recall them the following days…

Drinks are fairly expensive (beer €9 and spirits €12) but it's worth it to have an unusual, off-beat time that combines naffness, simplicity, and good humour. If it's too much, you can always go and have your demi at the bar out front (€4).

LA DIVETTE DE MONTMARTRE

136, rue Marcadet 75018 Paris
- Access: M° Jules-Joffrin
- Tel.: 01 46 06 19 64
- Open Tues-Thurs 3pm-1am, Fri-Mon 5pm-1am

The entire place is covered with vinyl records

From the outside, La Divette de Montmartre looks just like any other neighbourhood bar.

But once you go through the door, you realize that it's really something completely out of the ordinary.

The entire, and we do mean entire - walls, ceiling, and even the bar counter - place is covered with vinyl records of various types, all of which feature artwork. There are far too many to mention here, but if you make the effort to examine this collection closely, you'll be amazed by the inventiveness of the illustrations, the fine quality of some of the artwork, and the sheer variety of the singers and groups.

If the production of these very distinctive records was fairly common before the advent of the compact disc, they've become quite rare these days. Today, only some rap, house, and hard rock musicians continue this appealing practice, like Iron Maiden, who by virtue of producing two illustrated vinyl records each year, are practically the only contemporary group that merits any praise from Serge, the owner of the bar.

Serge started his collection about fifteen years ago. And barely a fifth of his holdings have found a place on the walls of his establishment. One finds among them notably two astonishing vinyl records with portraits of Pope John Paul II, one of them being a pirate version, an oversized vinyl bearing the picture of Mireille Mathieu in a duo with another equally big name, Patrick Duffy. And even if it's not illustrated, you should also check out a very curious record from the beginning of the 20th century: it runs at 120 or 130 rpm, a type which we're willing to bet that most of you were unaware even existed.

Finally, one other noteworthy feature that adds to the peculiarity of this surprising venue is owner Serge who is none other than Serge Foucault, the brother of the ineffable French television personality and game show host, Jean-Pierre Foucault…

STUDIO DES ISLETTES

10, rue des Islettes 75018 Paris
• Access: M° Barbès-Rochechouart
• Tel.: 01 42 58 63 33
• Open daily 9.30pm-12.30am, except Sundays.
• Instrumental jam sessions Mondays, Tuesdays, and Thursdays: Free
• Vocal jam sessions Wednesdays : €6
• Concerts Fridays and Saturdays: €10

*Intimate jazz
at Barbès*

L e Studio des Islettes is not really a bar, properly speaking. A small jazz club that opened about twenty years ago, it has managed happily to preserve itself from tourists and pretence, probably thanks in part to its unattractive location at the foot of the Goutte d'Or neighbourhood in the north of Paris.

But this venue is certainly worthwhile visiting. Patrick Irénée Tsciakpé, the head of the association that manages the place, has succeeded for many years in offering high-quality programmes while maintaining a particularly convivial atmosphere.

The initial impression is somewhat surprising. In a street running perpendicular to the boulevard de la Chapelle, an ordinary building identifies itself to the curious passer-by by a small trumpet next to an intercom. You ring, cross an inner courtyard, pass through a heavy door that ensures sound-proofing, and you're there.

Barely thirty seats are provided in front of a small stage. Jazz fans come and go as they please, and people converse in low verses. In this little musical paradise, one can, while respecting the musicians, have a quiet chat while drinking beer or red wine. You won't be able to tell your life story to a long-lost friend, but you will be able to spend a very pleasant time there.

ICE BAR - ICE KUBE

1-5 passage ruelle 75018 Paris
• Acces: M° Marx Dormoy
• Tel.: + 33 1 42 05 2000 . Fax: + 33 1 42 05 21 01
• www.kubehotel.com
• paris@kubehotel.com

> *At -5° C, your glass made of ice will slowly melt at the touch of your burning lips...*

Of course, this isn't the Ice Bar at the Ice Hotel in Swedish Lapland, right up near the Arctic Circle. But the idea is the same and it turns out that you can have a good time here, even if the place has become part of the trendy circuit in the French capital. Here's the set-up. First of all, you need to be motivated to venture into this rather dreary corner of the 18th arrondissement. Located near the Marx Dormoy Métro station, between the railway lines running into the Gare de l'Est and those leading to the Gare du Nord, the very least one can say is that the Ice Kube was a pioneer in establishing itself in the area. Our advice is to avoid going there on foot, which risks being a rather scary experience...

The first glimpse is surprising: facing onto a cul-de-sac, a handsome U-shaped building contains the hotel, the bar, and the restaurant. With its designer decor, the restaurant offers a very inventive and rather successful cuisine.

But the really interesting part is upstairs, at the Ice Bar. Reserve your entry time in advance (the bar's capacity is relatively limited), pay the 38 euros admission fee, put on the polar environment suit that is graciously provided, and you're now ready to penetrate into a space maintained at a constant temperature of -5° C.

With its bar made of ice, snow-covered floor, and walls also composed of ice, only the ceiling (sadly) is out of keeping with this arctic setting. Even the glasses

are carved from ice, with the rather startling result that your glass slowly begins to melt as it comes into contact with your burning lips...

The admission price gives you the right to consume, for the first 30 minutes, as much as you like of a large variety of vodkas... In the commendable spirit of turning the cost of the evening to best advantage, it's common practice for customers to down several shots of vodka in 5-10 minutes. Needless to say, the atmosphere soon becomes quite jovial. When you leave, try to sober up a little before wandering off into the neighbourhood...

THE BOX IN PARIS

Late-night meals, evening tastings, and buffet-style aperitifs at The Box in Paris gallery
Open Tues-Sat 3pm-8pm, and evenings when events are scheduled
6, cité du Midi, 75018 Paris • Access: Mo Pigalle
• Tel.: 01 42 51 52 42 • E-mail: contact@theboxinparis.com
• Programme: www.theboxinparis.com
• Prices: Late-night meal: main dish €15; evening tastings: €35, excluding drinks
• Guest room: bed and breakfast from €150

Dinner in a modern art loft-gallery

Various exhibition and living spaces are organised around a big box, hence the name: The Flavour Box, the kitchen, The Lab, the exhibition hall in the basement, as well as The White Box and The Black Box, two very beautiful guest rooms. As for Aline, simultaneously owner, gallery director, cook, and events organizer for this venue, she lives and works in her own separate quarters… The Private Box.

If the "concept" strikes you as a little pompous at first, don't be misled. Because this large and somewhat austere-looking loft turns out to be a warm and surprising place.

The originality of The Box lies in the proliferation of its nocturnal activities. Organised around photo exhibitions, the gallery comes to life with small concerts, readings, and gastronomic evenings. A sort of 21st-century dining hall, or a "rock 'n' roll" kind of place, as Aline puts it, where you find yourself opening up to total strangers with whom you have been merrily seated at the table.

The menu and the programming changes frequently but the spirit remains the same: somewhere between an arty meeting place and a neighbourhood cultural centre. If the dinners may seem a little expensive to some (€35), the originality and quality of an evening spent here make it well worth the price.

MOBILHOME

21, rue de la Mare 75020 Paris
- E-mail: mobilhome@noos.fr
- Open Wednesdays from 7pm.
- (Light) dinner: €6. Membership card: €5.

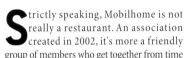

Kisses for dinner

Strictly speaking, Mobilhome is not really a restaurant. An association created in 2002, it's more a friendly group of members who get together from time to time, notably every Wednesday evening, when the association's premises serve as a bar-restaurant.

If this is your first visit, Coco explains the concept to you, you hand over €5 (or €2 towards the end of the year) in order to join the association, your picture is taken to immortalize the event, and you're all set. To put yourself in the right frame of mind, glance through the three binders that contain all the members' photos, and into which your own will soon be added.

The atmosphere is particularly warm, even familial. Everyone is chatting away, the music sounds good, and it's enjoyable watching three of the founders preparing dinner in front of us. The meal is served late, so we suggest that you nibble something beforehand if you don't want to wait until 10.30pm. That will also attenuate the effects of the numerous apéritifs that you'll end up drinking before the appointed hour.

To pay, you buy some kisses at the bar - these are simply pieces of paper with pairs of lips drawn on them - and order your drink. €2 for a glass of wine, €6 for the meal, the cost remains very reasonable, especially given the quality of the plate that is prepared for you. On the day we visited, the samosas, cream soup, and terrine were quite simply divine. No dessert, and it might be best not to arrive feeling too hungry at these get-togethers.

An unusual and particularly warm-hearted venue.

LA FERME DU BONHEUR

220, avenue de la République 92000 Nanterre
- Access : RER A Nanterre-Université
- la.ferme.du.bonheur@free.fr
- Tel.: 01 47 24 51 24
- Guest dining table open weekdays for lunch. Around €10

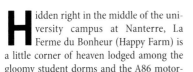

Alternative animals

Hidden right in the middle of the university campus at Nanterre, La Ferme du Bonheur (Happy Farm) is a little corner of heaven lodged among the gloomy student dorms and the A86 motorway. To get there, get out at the rear of the RER train from Paris, head toward the University and it's straight in front of you, as you walk alongside the tennis courts in the direction of some circus tents that you can't miss.

La Ferme has multiple uses: as one might expect, it shelters dogs, goats, chickens, rabbits, a pig, a donkey, and a horse, but there's also a makeshift theatre and a dining room for guests.

The place overflows with the simple joy of living attuned to others by applying the oft forgotten principle of Fraternity.

Set up here for twelve years now, Roger des Prés is a true man of the theatre, an ardent admirer notably of Jean Genet due to his choice of a life of total freedom. A choice that this loveable man is also trying to make, while

assuming overall responsibility for an installation that occupies several people full time. Between the plays that he produces regularly and the guest table, Roger hasn't opted for a selfish form of liberty but instead has become a man who shares.

For a modest amount, the guest table, installed in a fairground tent, constitutes the best way of absorbing the ambience of this inimitable place. Don't miss it. For employees working in the offices towers at La Défense, only five minutes away by RER, it's an alternative lunch spot that offers a change from the daily routine. Don't forget to remove your tie.

TABLE D'HÔTES DE L'ESPACE PRO-CAR

31, rue Parmentier 92800 Puteaux
• Access: M° Esplanade de La Défense or SNCF Puteaux station
• Tel./Fax. : 01 42 04 10 28
• Guest dining table open weekdays lunch time
• Dish of the day € 15

Lunch at a vintage car dealer's garage

As its name indicates, the Espace Pro-Car is devoted to the world of the automobile. Opened at the beginning of 2004, this venue is hidden in a quiet back street of old Puteaux. For the curious and hungry stroller, the place presents above all the astonishing feature of offering a very nice table d'hôtes (a dining table for paying guests).

Formerly a senior manager for a big electronics firm, Jacques Guérin decided one fine day to abandon all that and dedicate his time to his long-standing passion, vintage cars. Together with his wife Evelyne, who also took this opportunity to leave her job as a hairdresser, they opened this very beautiful space and at long last 'please themselves'.

A few months later, they were all set up. The welcome is charming and you eat well there. Everything is home-cooked by Evelyne who brings the dishes freshly prepared from their house.

There are already regular customers coming here, always a good sign, and you surprise yourself by spending two or three hours there, unaware of the passing time. And wind things up with a brief tour to view the latest acquisitions: a Jaguar type E, a Lancia Fulvia, and a Mercedes SL. Jacques has his own preferences and is visibly aiming at the collectors' market. The address is becoming known in the small world of vintage car fans. A recent four-page feature article in the French specialist magazine, Rétroviseur (Rear-View Mirror...) brought some customers, and not just for lunch.

LE RESTAURANT DE MAINS D'ŒUVRES

1, rue Charles-Garnier 93400 Saint-Ouen
- Access: M° Garibaldi or Porte-de-Clignancourt, or Bus 85, stop at Paul-Bert
- Open weekdays for lunch.
- Tel.: 01 40 11 25 25
- www.mainsdoeuvres.org

*Artists'
canteen*

Mains d'Oeuvres, just a short walk from the famous Saint-Ouen flea-market, needs no introduction to most Parisians. But those of you who have already attended its concert hall, may not know that you also have lunch there. Located in the same building, on the ground floor, the restaurant offers its clientele a perfectly kitsch decor. You'll be

welcomed by Jules and Chloé who propose, depending on the day and the season, a French cuisine using fresh produce, including plates of tartines, tarts, and salads. Their dish of the day generally cost €8. If you're really hungry, there's a choice between two fixed-price menus at €10 and €12 (tart-salad or a main dish, dessert, drink, and a coffee).

Mains d'œuvres is a venue for artistic creation and exhibition that also houses artists-in-residence. The building used to be the social and sports centre for the Valéo factory, before opening its space of 4,000 m^2 to the general public in January 2001.

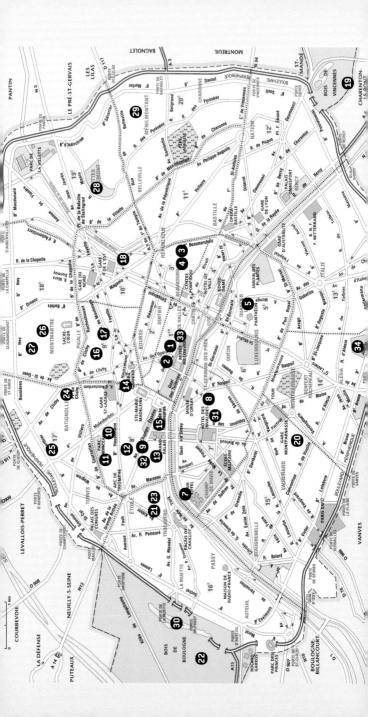

SECRET GARDENS AND OPEN-AIR TERRACES

CAFÉS DU MUSÉE DU LOUVRE

Musée du Louvre 75001 Paris
See p. 10

LE SAUT DU LOUP

Musée des Arts décoratifs
107, rue de Rivoli 75001 Pari. Métro Palais Royal-Musée du Louvre ou Tuileries.
• Tél. : 01 42 25 49 55 • www.lesautduloup.com
• Open daily 12am-7pm.
Very beautiful hidden terrace in the Tuileries garden.

ALTEA

41, rue Charlot 75003 Paris. Access: M° Filles-du-Calvaire
• Tél. : 01 42 77 71 00
• Open Tues-Sat 11am-8pm.
Mainly a shop selling tea, Altea also has a small, split-level terrace that's very pleasant on hot summer days, but rather sombre the rest of the time. It's always quiet, however, allowing you to have a peaceful cup of one of the many teas available, for around €3-€4 per pot.

PASSAGE DE RETZ

9, rue Charlot 75003 Paris. Access: M° Filles-du-Calvaire
• Open daily noon-7pm, except Mondays, during exhibitions
(very frequent, call for schedule).
Superb terrace in the cobbled inner courtyard of a handsome townhouse in the Marais neighbourhood. Completely invisible from the street, this small café offers, in an atmosphere of Olympian calm, fruit juices (€3), tea (€2.50), coffee (€2), and ice cream in the summer. Inside the building, there are four designer tables for when the weather is poor. Occupying the site of the former Fryd toy factory that was active from 1948 to 1980, the Passage de Retz is now a contemporary art gallery.

◀ CHANTAIRELLE

17, rue Laplace, 75005 Paris. Access: M° Cardinal-Lemoine
• Tél. : 01 46 33 18 59
• www.chantairelle.com
• Closed Saturday lunch time and Sundays.
Near the Panthéon, Chantairelle has a very pleasant garden terrace, invisible from the street. There is absolute calm amidst the greenery for the seven or eight tables set up outdoors. The food, copious but uneven in quality, has its roots in the region of Auvergne and more specifically the area around Puy-en-Velay, for which the restaurant, with its corner selling local produce and its brochures, is practically a Parisian embassy. Lentils, stuffed cabbage, viande de Salers, and (somewhat disappointing) truffades will subdue the most voracious appetites for prices that aren't exactly cheap: the main dishes range from €14 to €20. The lunch menus are more worthwhile at €14 and €18. There's also a refreshing moment when you enter the place, and set off a splendid and sonorous 'moo' from an Auvergnat cow.

CAFÉ BRANLY - RESTAURANT LES OMBRES

Café: in the gardens of the museum
37, quai Branly 75007 Paris
• Tél. : 01 47 53 68 01• www.quaibranly.fr
• Open Tuesday-Sunday 9am-6pm (8pm Thrursdays, Fridays, Saturdays).
Restaurant: Musée du quai Branly, Portail Alma
27, quai Branly 75007 Paris. Métro Pont-de-l'Alma
• Tél.: 01 47 53 68 00 • www.lesombres-restaurant.com
• Open daily 12am-2.30pm and 7.30pm-10.30pm (11pm Fridays and Saturdays)

Superb view of Paris and the Eiffel Tower in particular. Lunch fixed menu at an acceptable price, but dining à la carte in the evening is too expensive. Down below, the café has a terrace offering a truly calm haven.

◀ LA MAISON DE L'AMÉRIQUE LATINE

217, boulevard Saint-Germain 75007 Paris. Access: M° Solferino
• Tél. : 01 49 54 75 10 • Closed on weekends • Menu: €37.

One often forgets the existence of this extraordinary terrace looking out at the two formal gardens attached to this 18th century townhouse. A big mistake, because you have the perfect illusion here of dining somewhere in the (beautiful) countryside, difficult to match anywhere else in Paris.

BAR LE LUCIEN

Hôtel Fouquet's Barrière. 46, avenue George V 75008 Paris. Métro George-V
• Tél. : 01 40 69 60 61 • Open daily 4pm-2h30pm

Pleasant terrace on the first floor, invisible from the street. Regularly frequented by would-be VIPs.

LE MARCANDE

52, rue de Miromesnil 75008 Paris. Access: M° Miromesnil
• Open daily except Saturday lunch time and Sundays.
• Tél.: 01 42 65 19 14 • www.marcande.com

In the middle of a fairly active business district, the calm tree-shaded patio of Le Marcande restaurant is a little haven of peace. Undetectable from the street, the interior terrace has seven very delightful tables. The traditional French cuisine is artfully produced, but the rather chic style of this venue will be reflected in the bill: a menu with starter-main course for €33, or €39 when dessert is added. If ordering à la carte, expect to pay around €60.

LES SALONS DU PARC MONCEAU ⑪

8, rue Alfred-de-Vigny 75008 Paris. Access: M° Courcelles • Tél. : 01 46 22 25 39
See p. 46

HÔTEL LANCASTER ⑫

7, rue de Berri 75008 Paris. Access: M° George-V • Tél. : 01 40 76 40 18

Of all the luxury hotels in Paris, the Hôtel Lancaster is probably the most discreet and one of the most pleasant. The superb, contemporary-style inner courtyard and the exceptional quality of the cuisine created by chef Fabrice Salvador should ensure that this venue will not remain unnoticed for long, but one never knows… Better hurry here, in any case!

RESTAURANT DU PRESS CLUB DE FRANCE : « LES SIGNATURES »

8, rue Jean-Goujon 75008 Paris • Tél. : 01 40 74 64 94
• www.pressclub.fr • Open daily noon-2.30pm

Hidden within a building that is home to the Press Club de France (a meeting-place for professional journalists), but also the Hôtel Sofitel and the Maison des Centraliens (the graduates' association of the École Centrale de Paris), Les Signatures provides a very agreeable and very calm garden terrace on fine days. Main courses for €23, menus at €33, €36, and €45, it's a little expensive for what it is, but you're also paying for the setting. It's perfect, however, if you're on an expense account or a member of the Press Club: the latter have the right to a 30% reduction. On weekends, the bar menu is served and prices become much more reasonable: the main dish of the day costs €16.

FAUCHON

26, place de la Madeleine 75008 Paris. Access: M° Madeleine • Tel. tea bar: 01 47 42 93 74.
• Tea bar open daily 11.30am-6.30pm for the tea service and noon-3pm for lunch, except on Sundays

Located in a fairly noisy neighbourhood, Fauchon's bar à thé has a nice, very calm terrace on the first floor, which seems to be unknown to most people in the area. There are seven to eight tables, including one in the sunshine, grouped around a central skylight. Attentive service. At lunch, the menu for €23.50 includes a cold plate (€12.50 as an individual dish), pastry and green tea.

RESTAURANT DU MUSÉE DES BEAUX-ARTS - PETIT PALAIS

Avenue Winston Churchill 75008 Paris. Access: M° Champs-Elysées Clémenceau
• Open 10am-6pm, except Mondays • Tel.: 01 40 07 11 41

Hidden within the magnificent museum of the Petit-Palais, which has recently been admirably renovated, there is a truly wonderful cafeteria. Try to find a place at the 7 or 8 tables outside: they face a charming little interior garden. Divine!

MUSÉE DE LA VIE ROMANTIQUE

16, rue Chaptal 75009 Paris. Access: M° Pigalle • Tél. : 01 49 95 08 64
• Open lunch time and afternoons, when weather permits.

A tea-room sublimely tucked away in the magnificent inner courtyard of the Musée de la Vie Romantique, and serving remarkable pastries from Maison Bertrand. Just a few tables for those who know how to make the most of life. A rare calm address in this bustling urban neighbourhood.

HÔTEL-RESTAURANT AMOUR

8, rue Navarin 75009 Paris. Access: M° Pigalle or Saint-Georges
• Open daily for breakfast, lunch and dinner, except Monday lunch time.
• Around €25 euros per person.

Open in spring 2006, the Hôtel Amour offers a ravishing little garden in which it is extremely pleasant to spend some time. The service is very friendly, and the cuisine is both decent and up-to-date.

CAFÉ A MAJUSCULE

148, rue du Faubourg-Saint-Martin 75010 Paris. Access: M° Gare-de-l'Est
• Closed on Mondays. Open other weekdays 11am-7pm, weekends 2pm-7pm.
Recently renovated, the former Recollets convent henceforth contains the Maison de l'Architecture. If the latter is taking its time bringing its programme up to cruising speed, some clever people have already been quick to spot the terrace of the Café A Majuscule (Capital A - for Architecture). It is hidden from the street by high walls that also block off the sound of traffic. And it's a little paradise whenever the sun puts in an appearance. Light meals served, with salads for around €8, quiches €7. Don't forget to take a look at the very beautiful space in the former convent's chapel, just before the entrance, to the right.

LA CIPALE

51, avenue de Gravelle 75012 Paris. Access: M° Liberté • Tél. : 01 43 75 54 53
See p. 68

OM'ZAKI ⓴

76, rue de la Procession 75015 Paris. Access: M° Pernety • Tél. : 01 56 58 08 82
See p. 86

LES ARTS ㉑

9bis, avenue d'Iéna 75016 Paris. Access: M° Iéna
• Tél. : 01 40 69 27 53
• Closed on weekends
• Menus from €36.
Home of the 'Gadzarts' (the alumni association of the École Nationale des Arts et Métiers, or ENSAM) since 1925, this handsome townhouse built in 1892 also conceals from prying eyes in the street a very beautiful terrace restaurant that looks out onto a pleasant little garden. Chic but stilted ambience.

◄ BAR-RESTAURANT DU GOLF DU BOIS DE BOULOGNE ㉒

Hippodrome d'Auteuil 75016 Paris. Access: M° Porte-Auteuil
• Tél. : 01 44 30 70 00
See p. 76

RESTAURANT LE STÜBLI ㉓

Institut Goethe. 17, avenue d'Iéna 75116 Paris. Access: M° Iéna
• Tél. : 01 44 43 92 30
• Open weekdays 11am-7pm. Annual closure from 28 July to 15 August inclusive
The restaurant-cafeteria of Institut Goethe, has a very calm, hidden terrace, even if its charm is a little spoilt by the surrounding modern buildings. Just the thing for those who need some peace and quite, or have a sudden desire for apfelstrüdel.

L'ELDORADO

18, rue des Dames 75017 Paris. Access: M° Place-de-Clichy
- Tél. : 01 45 22 13 42

See p. 86

RESTAURANT « LES JARDINS D'AMPÈRE »

102, avenue de Villiers 75017 Paris. Access: M° Pereire.
- Tél. : 01 44 29 16 54
- Open daily noon-2pm and 7.30pm-10pm, except Sunday evenings.

Located within the Hôtel Ampère, a short walk from the place Pereire, Les Jardins d'Ampère sets out a few tables in front of a delightful little interior garden. Calm, greenery, menus at €28 and €38, and a rather classic French cuisine all make this a great deal, especially since the residents and employees in the neighbourhood rarely seem aware of its existence. So on fine days you can usually find a table here, even at the last minute…

LE VIEUX CHALET

14bis, rue Norvins. 75018 Paris. Access: M° Abbesses
- Tél. : 01 46 06 21 44
- Lunch served until 2.30pm and dinner until 9.30pm, except Sunday evenings and Mondays.

In the very heart of the tourist quarter of Montmartre, and a short distance from the place du Tertre, the inner courtyard of the Vieux Chalet seems like a small miracle preserved from the ravages of unbridled capitalism. A paradise for tourists and a lucky find for Parisians, it has nine tables set out in the vegetation around a central tree. Traditional French cuisine at reasonable prices (€12-€13 for main courses). As you enter, notice the ceiling, covered with hundreds of ancient matchboxes.

LE SQUARE

227bis, rue Marcadet 75018 Paris. Access: M° Guy-Môquet
- Tél. : 01 53 11 08 41
- Closed at lunch time on weekends, and on Sun-Mon evenings.

A pleasant neighbourhood restaurant. Good lunch menu (€13 starter plus main course, or main course plus dessert). A very nice garden terrace removed from noise and pollution.

ZABAR CAFÉ

116, rue de Ménilmontant 75020 Paris. Access: M° Gambetta
- Tél. : 01 46 36 60 20
- www.zabar.cafe.fr
- Open Tues-Sat lunch time and dinner.

Although the ownership changed hands at the end of 2004, it was the cook who took over, and the little garden terrace remains. A few tables, no noise, sunshine, enjoy.

AND OF COURSE, ALTHOUGH THEY ARE NOT AT ALL SECRET:

PAVILLON PUEBLA , CHEZ VINCENT

Parc des Buttes Chaumont. Entrée à l'angle de l'avenue Bolivar et de la rue Botzaris, 75019 Paris. Métro Buttes-Chaumont
- Tél. : 01 42 02 22 45
- Ouvert tous les jours sauf dimanche de 20h à 2h. Soirées musicales à partir d'avril 2008 à partir de 22h30.

The famous Pavillon Puebla has finally reopened. The terrace enjoys a degree of tranquility rarely to be found in Paris.

LE CHALET DES ILES

14, chemin de Ceinture-du-Lac-Inférieur 75016 Paris
- Tél. : 01 42 88 04 69
- Around €40.

Located on the island in the middle of the big lake within the Bois de Boulogne, the Chalet des Îles was renovated in 2001. A superb terrace where calm and tranquillity are guaranteed. Not a single car. But lots of trees, flowers, and chlorophyll.

CAFÉTÉRIA DU MUSÉE RODIN

77, rue de Varenne 75007 Paris
- Tél. : 01 44 18 61 10

Right in the middle of the museum's superb garden. But it's still a cafeteria, alas…

LE PERSHING HALL

49, rue Pierre-Charron 75008 Paris
- Tél. : 01 58 36 58 00

Despite the presence of the jet set and the prices, the patio with its extraordinary wall of greenery is a must.

CAFÉ MARLY

93, rue de Rivoli 75001 Paris
- Tél. : 01 49 26 06 60

A not-to-be-missed terrace with a view of the Louvre pyramid. Magical in the evenings, before going on to discover just a few steps away the no less magical Cour Carré, also best seen at night. Reserve ahead of time!

PAVILLON MONTSOURIS

20, rue Gazan 75014 Paris. In the Parc Montsouris. RER B line Cité-Universitaire.
- Tel.: 01 43 13 29 00. Around €50 per person.

A unique setting in Paris, a restaurant right in the middle of a public park.

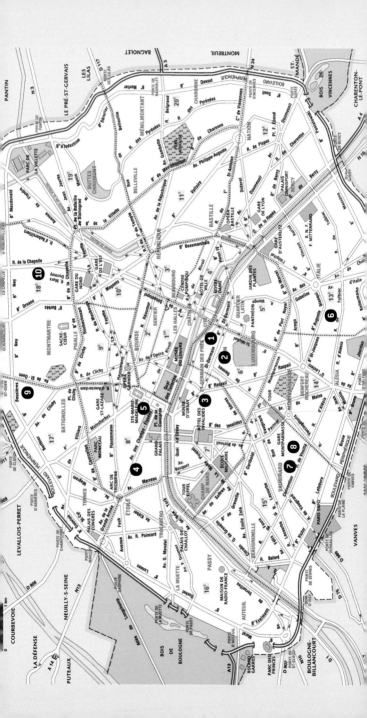

ROMANTIC

LAPÉROUSE

51 quai des Grands-Augustins 75006 Paris
• Tél. : 01 43 26 68 04

Worth visiting for the exceptional decor of its six small private salons, which date back to 1766. For those of you who are roguishly inclined, these salons are truly private: the waiter will only open the door if you call for him... You wouldn't be the first to let yourselves go in these rooms: when it first opened, this establishment was a favourite den of courtesans and their lovers. Be sure to note the scratches on certain mirrors: some of these young women of dubious virtue did not hesitate to quickly test the authenticity of the diamonds that they had just received as gifts... Dumas, Hugo, Zola, Flaubert, and Maupassant were all frequent visitors to this place. In more recent times, it has been rumoured that there was a tunnel leading here from the nearby restaurant of the French Senate. The senators were particularly appreciative of these premises for discreet encounters... Expensive (€50 to €100 per person) but refined cuisine.

◀ LE BAR

27, rue de Condé 75006 Paris. Access: M° Odéon
• Tél. : 01 43 29 06 61
See p. 38

LA MAISON DE L'AMÉRIQUE LATINE ❸

217, boulevard Saint-Germain 75007 Paris. Access: M° Solferino
• Tél. : 01 49 54 75 10
• Closed on weekends. Menu: €37.
See p. 127

JAIPUR - HÔTEL VERNET ❹

25, rue Vernet 75008 Paris
• Tél. : 01 44 31 98 06
• Open daily noon-2.30pm and 6pm-11.30pm.

In the cellars of the Hôtel Vernet, just to the left of the entrance, the Jaipur restaurant is a cosy address unknown to most Parisians. A boudoir in a romantic decorative style that recalls former colonial outposts in the East Indies, this very warm setting is filled with the scent of a sweet, almost intoxicating incense.

The deep sofas and the quiet charm will incite couples to while away long hours here... Cocktails for €15 and a main course of the day for €18 will permit you to prolong the moment. If the magic really works its spell, there will still be time to take a room in the hotel just above...

Rates start at €210 per night for a double room.

1728

8, rue d'Anjou 75008 Paris. Access: M° Concorde
- Tél. : 01 40 17 04 77
- Restaurant open noon-2.30pm and 8pm-11pm. Tea served 3pm-7pm, cocktails 6pm-8pm. à 19h. Cocktail de 18h à 20h.
- Average price: €50.

A magical spot in the evenings for a romantic dinner, in an atmosphere that's both refined and completely out of the ordinary. The quiet, cosy setting lets you adrift from the bustling modern city outside to plunge three hundred years back in time.

1728 is simply the year in which this Parisian townhouse was built. Rich in history, the place was a great favourite of the courtiers in Madame de Pompadour's entourage, and its most famous guest was no doubt La Fayette.

Every Saturday, from 4pm to 6pm, 1728 takes up the tradition of the 18th century cultural and literary salons, proposing an exchange with an artist, an author, or an expert in connection with a work of art on sale in the salon, a book that has just been published, or a concert.

BANGKOK THAÏLANDE

35, boulevard Auguste-Blanqui 75013 Paris. Access: M° Corvisart or Place-d'Italie
- Tél. : 01 45 80 76 59
- Closed Sundays and Monday lunch time.
See p. 60

◂ VILLA TOSCANE

36-38, rue des Volontaires 75015 Paris. Access: M° Volontaires
- Tél. : 01 43 06 82 92
- Closed Saturday lunch time and Sundays. Menu: €27.
See p. 70

OM'ZAKI

76, rue de la Procession 75015 Paris. Access: M° Pernety or Plaisance
- Tel.: 01 56 58 08 82.
- Open daily except Saturday lunch time and Sundays.
See p. 72

COMPTOIR 1900

12, rue Arthur-Brière 75017 Paris. Access: M° Guy-Môquet.
- Tél. : 01 42 28 16 06
See p. 96

CHEZ ARSÈNE ❿

12, rue Doudeauville 75018 Paris. Access: M° Marx-Dormoy.
- Tél. : 01 46 07 46 32
See p. 97

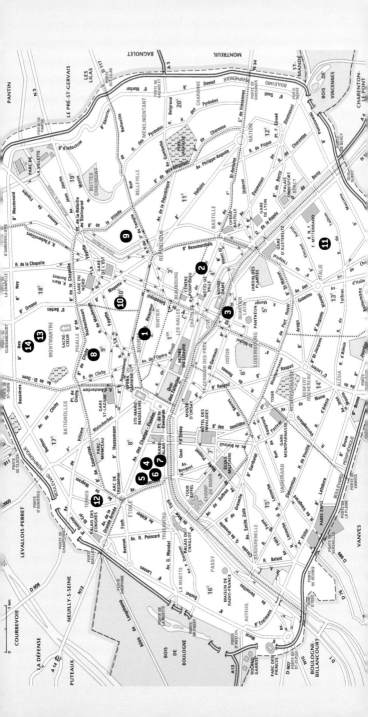

ATYPICAL FOODS

Haricots de mer au naturel
Judía de mar al natural

Ingredients : Haricots de mer, eau, sel marin, extrait de citron.
Conseil d'utilisation : Rincer à l'eau avant utilisation.
Idée recette : Haricots de mer à la poêle - Faire revenir dans le beurre
oignons, échalotes ou ail et poêler les haricots de mer pendant 1 ou 2
minutes.

Ingredientes : Judía de mar, agua, sal de mar, extracto de limon.
Consejos para consumo : Enjuagar previamente en agua
Idea de receta : Judía de mar a la sarten. Revenir suavemente en un poco
de mantequilla, cebollas, echalotas o ajo, y agragar los frejoles de mar
durante 1 o 2 minutos.

Date limite de consommation
voir sur le couvercle

Poids Net Egoutte : 400 gr
Poids Net Total : 700 gr

ALGUE SERVICE
ZI de Bloscon - F29680 ROSCOFF
www.algue-service.com

3 545 45 056 900 7

MALABAR ICE CREAM - Café Moderne

40, rue Notre-Dame-des-Victoires 75002 Paris. Access: M° Bourse
- Tél. : 01 53 40 84 10
- Open daily, except Sundays.
- Lunch menus: €24 and €29.

Please note that the Malabar (a French brand of bubble-gum) ice cream isn't always on the menu, but it does exist, just ask for it.

SEAWEED SALAD - Piccolo Teatro

6, rue des Ecouffes 75004 Paris. Access: M° Saint-Paul
- Tél. : 01 42 72 17 79
- Open daily lunch time and evenings.

A nice restaurant that offers, in addition to the seaweed salad, another type of seaweed in its vegetarian plate.

CURDLED BLOOD - Pho 67

67, rue Galande 75005 Paris. Access: M° Maubert-Mutualité
- Tél. : 01 43 25 56 69
- Open daily lunch time and evenings.

The curdled blood isn't always on the menu, so it's best to phone and order it in advance. For €8, you can try this Vietnamese dish made from pork blood, mint, and lemons, and which looks like jelly. An indescribable and incomparable taste. For the curious-minded.

MALABAR ICE CREAM
AND TAGADA STRAWBERRY ICE CREAM - Spoon

14, rue Marignan 75008 Paris. Access: M° Franklin-Roosevelt
- Tél. : 01 40 76 34 44
- www.spoon.tm.fr
- Open weekdays.

Malabar and also Tagada strawberry ice creams available for €12.50 per helping, but they're made by French chef Alain Ducasse and his students of fine cuisine.

NUTELLA ICE CREAM - Flora

36, avenue George-V 75008 Paris . Access: M° George-V
- Tél. : 01 40 70 10 49.
- Open daily noon-2.30pm and 7pm-11pm, except Saturday lunch time and Sundays.

More precisely entitled 'Chaud-froid de chocolat et glace Nutella, churros à tremper' (we make that out to be hot chocolate and cold Nutella ice cream, with Spanish fried dough sticks for dunkin', quite a mouthful!), Flora's dessert using this French brand of nut spread does not have a pronounced Nutella taste, but it's good, as is everything in this place. And good value for money, too, with starter-main course-dessert for €34.

CARAMBAR, NUTELLA, AND TAGADA STRAWBERRY MACAROONS - Relais Plaza

21, avenue Montaigne 75008 Paris. Access: M° Alma-Marceau
• Tél. : 01 53 67 64 00
• Open daily.
• Menu: €43

If you want to avoid paying this steep bill, the owner sometimes agrees to let you have order coffee (€5), with the macaroons as an extra dainty treat.

COCKTAIL BUBBLE-GUM - Bar du Plaza-Athénée

25, avenue Montaigne 75008 Paris. Access: M° Alma-Marceau
• Tél. : 01 53 67 66 00
• Open daily 6pm-1.30am

The highly creative bartenders at the most hyped-up bar in Paris have come up with this surprising cocktail. Not to be missed, while admiring the pretty girls and attractive decor by a student of French designer Philippe Starck.

◀ GRAIN JUICE - Pousse Pousse

7, rue Notre-Dame-de-Lorette 75009 Paris. Access: M° Notre-Dame-de-Lorette
• Tél. : 01 53 16 10 81
• Open Tues-Fri 11am-3.30pm and 4.30pm-7.30pm., Saturdays 11am-6pm.

More of an organic food shop and juice bar than a veritable bar or restaurant, Pousse Pousse offers an astonishing grain juice (€5, and 5pm-7pm: only €2.50). The plants used are grown on the spot using épeautre (einkorn, an archaic form of wheat), barley, and kamut (another ancient grain), sometimes called the 'wheat of the Pharaohs' cut before your very eyes and then pressed into juice. Peculiar, but very good for your health!

COUTANCIE BEEF - Ploum

20, rue Alibert 75010 Paris. Access: M° Goncourt or République
• Tél. : 01 42 00 11 90.
• Closed Sundays and Mondays

A friendly restaurant with Japanese leanings, Ploum has the special distinction of being, to our knowledge, the only restaurant in Paris that offers Coutancie beef. Courtesy of their butcher located in the nearby rue Beaurepaire, one of the few places in the city where you buy this exceptional meat. At the restaurant, for €22, you can enjoy a slice of the best quality beef in France, and somewhat similar to Kobe beef in Japan. The animal's appetite is whetted with three litres of beer per day, which also encourages marbling and adds flavour to the meat. A daily massage ensures the dispersal of fat, favours the development of the dorsal muscles, and increases relaxation. With individual stalls to reduce stress caused by the aggressiveness of stable-mates, nothing is too good for these steers whose meat can be purchased from about €30 per kilo at the butcher's shop.Here's the address of another butcher who supplies this kind of beef: Boucherie Barone, 6, rue du Marché-Saint-Honoré.

TIRAMISU AU CARAMBAR - Café Panique

12, rue des Messageries 75010 Paris. Access: M° Poissonnière
- Tél. : 01 47 70 06 84
- Open weekdays.
- Evening menu: €29.

Hidden at the end of a building corridor, Café Panique is a most original venue. Its owner can be a little pretentious at times, but she's no publicity seeker. A very beautiful glass-roofed space that occupies the building's former courtyard, and offering a delicious tiramisu au Carambar (a chewy caramel).

FISH BLADDER - La Mer de Chine

159, rue du Château-des-Rentiers 75013 Paris. Access: M° Nationale
- Tél. : 01 45 84 22 49
- Open daily, lunch time and evenings, except Tuesdays.

For starters at €6 and €14.50 as a main dish, you'll have the astonishing privilege of eating fish bladder. Mixed in with crab meat, it comes in the form of a soup. Try some, but of course…

CROCODILE AND HEDGEHOG - Gazelle ⓬

9, rue Rennequin 75017 Paris. Access: M° Ternes.
- Tél. : 01 42 67 64 18
- Open weekdays lunch time and evenings, as well as Saturday evenings..
- Menus from €14.50 .

If you don't look like the police and ask politely, this Cameroonian restaurant will perhaps serve you crocodile or hedgehog, specialities from the country of tennis player Yannick Noah. But beware, these dishes are illegal in France, and so you obviously won't find them on the menu.

SEAWEED PIZZA AND SEAWEED PANCAKES - Le Pend'art ⓭

14, rue du Ruisseau 75018 Paris. Access: M° Lamarck
- Tél. : 01 42 62 06 72
- Open daily in the evenings, and Sunday noon for brunch

The seaweed pizza (€11), or to be more precise, made with 'haricots de la mer' (buttonweed) is very good, even though the taste of seaweed is not very pronounced. There's also seaweed pancakes for €9.50.

SNAKE LIQUEUR - Le Petit Ornano

72, boulevard d'Ornano 75018 Paris
- Open daily 8am-11pm

If you manage to convince the indefatigable lady who owns this venue to serve you up some of her old-fashioned snake liqueur, you'll earn our undying respect. Barfly ambience out of another era.

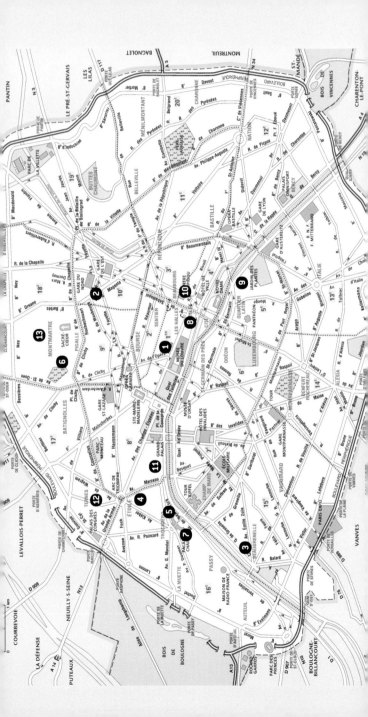

EXTRAORDINARY VIEWS

3 UNKNOWN CAFES AT LE LOUVRE MUSEUM ❶

Musée du Louvre 75001 Paris
See p. 10

CAFÉTÉRIA DU CENTRE COMMUNAUTAIRE ❷
JUIF DE PARIS

119, rue Lafayette 75010 Paris. Access: M° Gare-du-Nord
• Tél. : 01 53 20 52 71
See p. 54

BENKAY ❸

Hôtel Novotel Beaugrenelle. 61, quai de Grenelle 75015 Paris. Access: M° Bir-Hakeim
• Tél. : 01 40 58 21 26
• Open daily. Menus: € 32- € 115
Expensive but good Japanese restaurant. Beautiful view, especially of the city lights at night, facing the Seine river.

LES JARDINS PLEIN CIEL. ❹
LE BAR DE L'HÔTEL RAPHAËL

17, avenue Kleber 75116 Paris. Access: M° Kléber or Charles-de-Gaulle-Étoile
• Tél. : 01 53 64 32 00. Fax : 01 53 64 32 02
• www.raphael-hotel.com - E-mail : banqueting@raphael-hotel.com
In the very chic Hôtel Raphaël, the English-style bar is everything you might hope for. Deep armchairs in a warm British atmosphere that encourages tranquil discussions with other patrons. But if the bar is very cosy, its really original feature lies elsewhere: look closely to your left just before you enter. Now, who wouldn't be proud to own this genuine painting by Turner that many museums would love to exhibit? And that's not all. You should also go upstairs to the terrace to enjoy a splendid view of the place de l'Étoile. And eventually, play the giant chess game laid out in the garden next to you.

◀ CAFÉ-RESTAURANT DU PALAIS DE CHAILLOT ❺

Théâtre de Chaillot 75016 Paris. Access: M° Trocadéro
See p. 84

TERRASS HÔTEL ❻

17, rue Joseph-de-Maistre 75018 Paris. Access: M° Abbesses
• Tél. : 01 46 06 72 85
• Open daily lunch time and evenings, from April to September when weather permits.
• Around €50 per person.
The only really interesting feature of this hotel is the 7th floor. To the right of the reception, a lift takes you up to one of the most beautiful terraces in Paris. Directly in front of you is the Eiffel Tower, and next to it the Invalides and the Musée d'Orsay. Just at your feet lies the Montmartre cemetery. The view alone is worth the visit. But the restaurant less so, unfortunately. It's not cheap (around €50 per person) and of only average quality. Still, it's perfect for taking a visiting client or that cousin just over from the States who will no doubt be thoroughly impressed by your knowledge of this 'secret' place.

AND OF COURSE, ALTHOUGH THEY ARE BY NO MEANS SECRET:

LE CAFÉ DE L'HOMME

Palais de Chaillot, enceinte du musée de l'Homme. 17, place du Trocadéro 75116 Paris
• Tél. : 01 44 05 30 15
The former Totem has kept its superb view.

KONG

1, rue du Pont-Neuf 75001 Paris. Access: M° Pont-Neuf.
• Tél. 01 40 39 09 00
Beautiful view, trendy decor by Philippe Starck.

ZYRIAB

9th floor of IMA 1, rue des Fossés-Saint-Bernard 75005 Paris. M° Jussieu.
• Tél. 01 53 10 10 20
• Closed Sunday evenings and Mondays.
Magnificent view, but somewhat spoiled by the mediocre food. Best for taking afternoon tea on a fine day.

GEORGES

6th floor of Centre Pompidou. 19, rue Beaubourg 75004 Paris. M° Rambuteau
• Tél. : 01 44 78 47 99
• Closed Tuesdays.
If you manage to find a table. Superb futurist decor, superb view, superb wome. Jet set.

MAISON BLANCHE

15, avenue Montaigne 75008 Paris. M° Alma-Marceau
• Tél. : 01 47 23 55 99
Chic and expensive, menu €65.

BAR PLEIN CIEL

3, place du Général-Koenig 75017 Paris
• Tél. : 01 40 68 51 31
From the 33rd floor of the Hôtel Concorde Lafayette, the view simply has to be spectacular…

R.

8, rue de la Cavalerie 75015 Paris. M° La Motte-Picquet-Grenelle
• Tél. : 01 45 67 06 85
Trendy.

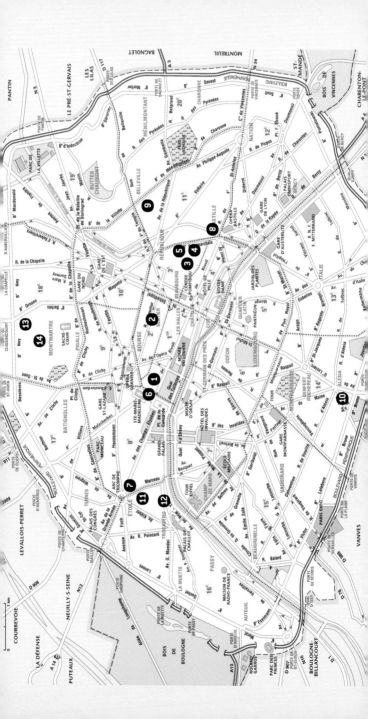

STARTLING TOILETS

LESCURE - 3rd on the right

7, rue Mondovi 75001 Paris. Access: M° Concorde
• Tél. : 01 42 60 18 91
• Open Mon-Fri noon-14.15pm and 7pm-10.15pm

A mainstay of Parisian life, Lescure proposes a traditional cuisine with rustic roots in the Limousin region. Main dishes for around €20. But Lescure also offers the curious the peculiarity of having its toilets outside the restaurant. Not in the courtyard like many establishments, but quite simply 20 metres away, along the same pavement. 'Down the street, third door on the right,' as the waiters will inform you!

LE LOUP BLANC - Nota bene

42, rue Tiquetonne 75002 Paris. Access: M° Les Halles
• Tél. : 01 40 13 08 35
• Open evenings from 7.30pm and Sunday lunch time.

Toilets where there's always a little pad of Post-Its lying about, plus a biro, to write down your immortal thoughts or a message of the moment. The mirror opposite is ideal as a sticking surface, so that they can be read by the next patrons to take their turn on the bowl.

RAIDD BAR - Keep cool

23, rue du Temple 75003 Paris. Access: M° Rambuteau
• www.raiddbar.com
See p. 18

LE TRÉSOR -
A goldfish in every flush

7, rue du Trésor 75004 Paris. Access: M° Saint-Paul
• Tél. : 01 42 71 35 17

A highly successful special effect. More than one customer has no doubt been caught wondering dazedly whether the poor fish swimming in the transparent tank is going to die in the sewers of Paris if they pull the chain! In fact, only half the water empties, and the fish remain perfectly safe in their glass home.

L'ÉTOILE MANQUANTE -
Outer space & postal train

34, rue Vieille-du-Temple 75004 Paris. Access: M° Saint-Paul
• Tél. : 01 42 72 48 34
• www.cafeine.com
• Open daily 9am-2am.

An appealing hetero café in the Marais, L'Etoile Manquante is of interest above all because of its toilets. A very effective spatial decor greets you on the ceiling. Once you've settled in the cabin, there's a very realistically rendered illusion of being watched by the residents living in a building facing you. And upon leaving, a camera films you washing your hand. Finally, a toy train running back and forth between the men's and women's toilets also permits you to send a possibly risqué note.

TOILETTES DE LA MADELEINE -
Art nouveau toilets

Place de la Madeleine 75008 Paris. Access: M° Madeleine
• Open daily 9.30am- 11h30am and 12.30pm-6.45pm

Even if they're not located in a bar or restaurant, we couldn't resist the desire
to mention the toilettes de la Madeleine, probably the most beautiful public
WCs in Paris. Built in 1905 by the Établissements Porcher, they are typically
Art Nouveau.

DRUGSTORE PUBLICIS -
Transparent toilets

133 avenue des Champs-Elysées 75008 Paris. Access: M° Charles-de-Gaulle-Étoile
• Tél : 33(0)1 44 43 79 00

Like the Belga Queen restaurant in Brussels (see Secret Brussels in this same
collection of guides), the Drugstore Publicis has some amazing toilets with
transparent doors down in the basement.

LE LÈCHE VIN -
Piety and pornography

13, rue Daval 75011 Paris. Access: M° Bastille
• Open evenings until 1.30am.

Religious objects fill the barroom proper. But when you get to the loo, you're
greeted by pornographic images, including some further adventures of Tintin…

L'AUTRE CAFÉ - Face-to-face

62, rue Jean-Pierre-Timbaud 75011 Paris. Access: M° Parmentier
• Tél. : 01 40 21 03 07
• Open weekdays 10am-2am, weekends 11.30am-2am.

After relieving yourself, you approach the basin to wash your hands as you
usually do. Surprise! Instead of the mirror for restoring order to your tousled
mane, you find yourself staring straight into the eyes of the stranger using the
toilet of the opposing sex. A good way to make contact…

◀ AUTO PASSION - Buckle up! !

⑩

197, boulevard Brune 75014 Paris. Access: M° Porte-d'Orléans
• Tél. : 01 45 43 20 20
See p. 66

BACCARAT - Mirrors, mirrors...

11, place des États-Unis 75116 Paris. Access: M° Kléber
• Tél. : 01 40 22 11 22
• Open Mon-Fri 10am-9pm, Saturdays 10am-7pm

In this very striking townhouse sublimely decorated by Philippe Starck, everything is a treat to the eye. If you don't know it yet, go and see for yourselves, even the boutique looks like a museum. But people often forget to make a trip to the toilets that are nevertheless well worth the visit. In the mirrors that completely cover walls and ceilings, your image quickly regresses into the infinite…
A perplexing perspective.

TOKYO EAT - Toilets for two

13, avenue du Président-Wilson 75016 Paris. Access: M° Iéna or Alma-Marceau
• Tél. : 01 47 20 00 29
• Open daily noon-3.30pm and 8pm-11.30pm (last orders), except on Mondays.

It's not much talked about because the rest of this place speaks for itself, but the toilets at Tokyo Eat are among the most original and surprising in the capital. So don't forget to have a look, before or after your meal. Upstairs, three very contemporary toilets reward the desires of the curious. For starters, they're all twin seaters. One finds toilets for children, urinals with a door (!), and almost classic models but with cleansing seats, like they have in Japan. In short there's something for every taste. As you leave, glance through one of several peepholes set in the translucent wall that separates the lavatory space from the main room. It's always useful to check on what your friends get up to when you're not around…Efficient, friendly service. Beforehand, while waiting for those same friends of yours to show up, the bookshop at the nearby Palais de Tokyo is recommended. For the more inquisitive, at the rear of the dining room you'll notice that outside beneath the two windows there are some nice little collective vegetable gardens. You'll find them again by exiting to the left and taking the stairs leading to the rue de la Manutention.

LA CASSEROLE - Photos, brassieres, and garter-belts

17, rue Boinod 75018 Paris. Access: M° Poissonnière
• Tél. : 01 42 54 50 97
• Closed on Sundays, Mondays, and Saturday lunch time.

July 2004: for safety reasons, the owner of La Casserole was forced to take down the incredible bric-à-brac that had been hanging from the ceiling for years. Happily, the toilets remain. Take your time examining the decor, no one will think twice about it… Countless erotic or pornographic photos, brassieres, panties, and garter-belts adorn every inch of the walls and ceiling. This exhibit has made the health & safety inspectors smile when they saw it …

LE PEND'ART - BD on display

14, rue du Ruisseau 75018 Paris. Access: M° Lamarck
• Tél. : 01 42 62 06 72
• Open evenings and Sundays for brunch.

By the kitchens, the toilets at the Pend'art are a hymn to bande dessinée. All of the walls and the ceiling are covered with panels from a BD entitled, 'The Adventures of Iggy' (meaning Iggy Pop), by an author who's a friend of the owner. They're now trying to getting this work published as an album…

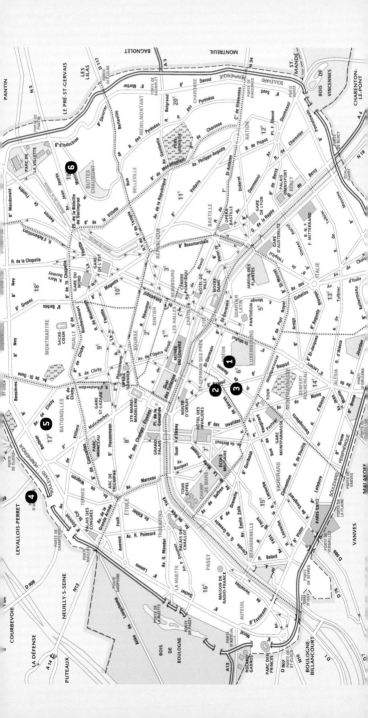

HOSTELRY SCHOOLS

VALUE FOR MONEY THAT'S DIFFICULT TO BEAT

Beyond the fun side of being served by student-waiters, the most interesting aspect of the training restaurants operated by the hostelry schools is the value for money they offer: the cooks and waiters are all students (under the close supervision of their instructors!), which means that these establishments do not have to pay the usual wage costs that are borne by other restaurants. But on the down side, they are prohibited from advertising (outside in the street, there is no sign or notice that even indicates the existence of a restaurant) and they remain closed from mid-May to September, while their students are on holidays... Also, it is best to go towards the end of the school year, when the apprentice cooks and waiters have acquired several months of experience...

ÉCOLE GRÉGOIRE-FERRANDI -
RESTAURANT QUATRIÈME

28, rue de l'Abbé-Grégoire 75006 Paris. Access: M° Saint-Placide, Sèvres-Babylone, or Vaneau
• Open weekly at lunch time and Thursday evenings
• Menus: €18, €22, and €35
• Reservations, call 01 49 54 17 31 and ask for Hatchi, Mon-Fri 8am-5pm.

The oldest of the Parisian restaurant schools, and its clientele is probably the most advanced in years as well... It has a delicious provincial atmosphere, with a fascinating mix of formality offset by the earnest amateurism of the waiters, an elegant but somewhat dated decor, and a maître d'hotel-instructor who trains his students with a deadpan sense of humour and has visibly made himself a favourite confidant of the amused customers.

LA TABLE D'ALBERT

3, rue Pierre Leroux. Access: M° Vaneau
• Tél. : 01 43 06 33 09
• Open for lunch and dinner, Tues-Thurs.

LYCÉE HÔTELIER JEAN QUARRÉ - GUILLAUME TIREL

237, boulevard Raspail 75014 Paris. Access: M° Raspail
• Tél. : 01 44 84 19 30
• New location since 10 July 2006.

ÉCOLE DE PARIS DES MÉTIERS DE LA TABLE, ❹
DU TOURISME ET DE L'HÔTELLERIE

17, rue Jacques-Ibert 75017 Paris. Access: M° Louise-Michel or Porte-de-Champerret
• Reservations, call 01 44 09 12 16, from 10.30-11.30am or 12.30-3pm.
• Open 12.30-2.30pm, Mon-Fri.
• Menus: €10 and €13.

Located at the city's border with the suburb of Levallois, beyond the Périphérique motorway, the training restaurant attached to the hostelry school in the rue Jacques-Ibert exhibits little charm, either on the outside of its building or in its interior decoration. But the particularly good value for money of its menu nevertheless makes a visit worthwhile.

INSTITUT VATEL ❺

122, rue Nollet 75017 Paris. Access: M° Brochant
• Tél. : 01 42 26 26 60
See page 94

CEPROC (CENTRE DE FORMATION ❻
DES PROFESSIONNELS DE LA CHARCUTERIE)

19, rue Goubet 75019 Paris. Access: M° Ourcq
• Tél.: 01 42 39 19 64. Reservations 72 hrs in advance.
• Open lunch time Mon-Fri.
• Lunch menu: €25 (including wine and coffee).
• www.ceproc.com

Located in a rather dismal corner of the 19th arrondissement, the CEPROC hostelry school serves meals on weekdays to gastronomes in the neighbourhood. Contrary to what its name suggests, this eatery offers other dishes besides cooked meats.

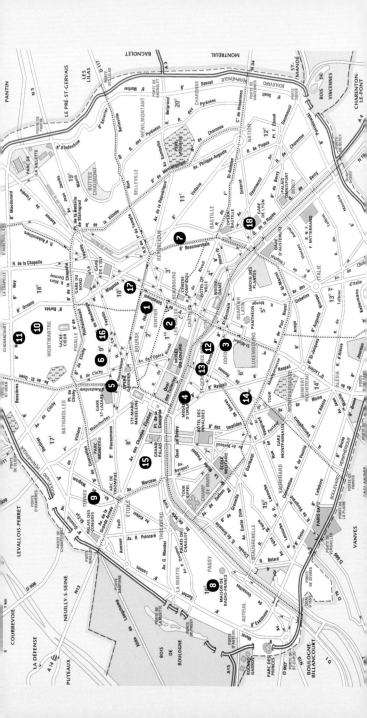

ART NOUVEAU / 1900

BAR-RESTAURANT LE ROYAL BAR

143, rue Saint-Denis 75002 Paris. Access: Mᵒ Réaumur-Rambuteau
- Tél. : 01 40 13 04 64. Open daily 10am-2am.
- Lunch 12am-5pm. Dinner possible by request.

Stuck in the middle of the sex shops along the rue Saint-Denis, Le Royal Bar offers the passing aesthete a superb and little-known decor made of ceramic tiles dating back to 1870. On the façade, the tiles to either side of the door spell out the names of apéritifs: vermouth, Martini. Inside the front room, just by the entrance, other tile displays promote the merits of four Italian regions, Lombardy, Latium, Veneto, and Piedmont. The tiles, entirely covering the walls except for the mirrors, are very beautiful and in very good condition. The other room to the rear is less interesting. But unfortunately, not much is known about these ceramics, except that the entire venue was listed as a protected site in 1999.

On fine days, the little terrace outside permits you to have a drink or one of the dishes of the day while enjoying the lively activity in the street. The cuisine is inexpensive (dish of the day: €8.50, menus: €9, €11, and €12) and unpretentious, but of good quality.

LE COCHON À L'OREILLE

15, rue Montmartre 75002 Paris. Access: RER Châtelet-Les Halles
- Tél. : 01 42 36 07 56
- Open daily 6am-midnight, except on Sundays.
- Lunch starting from around €15.

Superb ceramic tile decorations from 1914, on the theme of the former glories of Les Halles wholesale market, which used to be only a short distance away. Traditional French cuisine.

BOUILLON RACINE

3, rue Racine 75006 Paris. Access: RER Luxembourg
- Tél. : 01 44 32 15 60
- www.bouillonracine.com
- Menus: €15.50 to €26.
- Open daily lunch time and evenings.

Beautiful Art Nouveau decor dating from 1906. Traditional French cuisine.

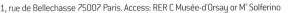

◢ RESTAURANT 1900 - MUSÉE D'ORSAY   ❹

1, rue de Bellechasse 75007 Paris. Access: RER C Musée-d'Orsay or M° Solferino
- Tél. : 01 45 49 47 03
- Open daily lunch time, except on Tuesdays, and also open Thursday evenings.
- Menus from €14.90.

This magnificent restaurant dining room, that of the former Orsay train station, remains curiously unfamiliar to Parisians. And yet it has a stunning 1900 decor. Ceilings painted by Gabriel Ferrier (1847-1914), mouldings, gilt, chandeliers, it has it all. The food is reasonable.

MOLLARD   ❺

115, rue Saint-Lazare 75008 Paris. Access: M° Saint-Lazare
- Tél. : 01 43 87 50 22
- www.mollard.fr
- Open daily noon-12.30am. Uninterrupted service.

Surprisingly, Parisians remain in the dark about this splendid brasserie opened in 1895. It's all the more a pity because the Art Nouveau setting created by Edouard Niermanns with the help of mosaicists and master glaziers is splendid. The Sarreguemines pottery works specially designed the original motifs representing allegorical figures and scenes from the end of the 19th century. Very decent cuisine at reasonable prices. Main dishes from €15.

CAFÉ FLO - LA COUPOLE DU PRINTEMPS   ❻

64, boulevard Haussmann 75009 Paris. Access: RER Auber or M° Havre-Caumartin
- Open daily lunch time and Thursday evenings only until 10pm.

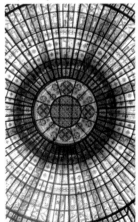

Another venue that has failed to register on most Parisians' radars, the Café Flo has the immense virtue of sheltering under the magnificent coupola of the Printemps department store, carried out by the master glazier Brière in 1923. It is composed of 3,185 glass panels, and measures 16 metres in height for a diameter of 20 metres. Due to the risk of being bombed by the Germans, it was dismantled in 1939 and put into storage in a warehouse in Clichy. It was not restored to its proper place until 1973, according to the instructions supplied by the grandson of Brière, who had kept the original plans in the family's workshop. The café's ambience today is unfortunately more that of a cafeteria than a restaurant. Lunch menu: €13.90, main courses à la carte around €15. Typical cuisine from Café Flo, that is to say, very run-of-the-mill.

LE CLOWN BAR

114, rue Amelot 75011 Paris. Access: M° Filles-du-Calvaire.
- Tél. : 01 43 55 87 35
- Open daily from 7pm.

One of the most beautiful settings in ceramic tile to be found in Paris, produced in 1919 at Sarreguemines. With reference to the nearby Cirque d'Hiver, the tiles represent the theme of the circus and clowns. The archives of this ceramic factory in eastern France having been burned during the Second World War, the exact identity of the author of these superb tiles remains unknown. Nevertheless, legend has it that he signed his work underneath the decor itself. But so far, the owner has never dismantled the tiles to elucidate the enigma…

CAFÉ ANTOINE

17, rue La Fontaine 75016 Paris . Access: M° Jasmin or RER C Avenue-du-Président-Kennedy.
- Tél. : 01 40 50 14 30
- Open daily 7.30am-11pm, except Sundays.

Located in a building constructed in 1911 by Hector Guimard, the leading proponent of Art Nouveau in France, Café Antoine opened in 1913. Named after the original owner, it then passed into the hands of her daughter who ran the establishment until 1996, when she was well into her eighties! With just two owners in 83 years, it's a fine example of longevity outstripping passing fashions! Since 1996, the new proprietor has turned it into an agreeable little restaurant with traditional French cuisine whose quality and prices are more than reasonable. One small surprise, however: if the external façade is typically Art Nouveau, the interior is more in a 1930s style. with superb floor tiling and paintings on canvasses and under glass, hung both on the side walls and on the ceiling.

LES GOURMETS DES TERNES

87, boulevard de Courcelles 75017 Paris. Access: M° Ternes
- Tél. : 01 42 27 43 04
- Closed Saturdays and Sundays.

This venerable bistro-style establishment provides ceramics lovers with a very beautiful example of ceramic tiles designed by Hyppolite Boulanger in 1880 and produced at the workshops of Choisy-le-Roi. The main panel portrays pink flamingos bracketed on either side by the symbols of commerce and industry. But those for crafts and agriculture are missing here. In fact, the tiles weren't originally here, but transferred in 1970 from the Chope Saint-Germain restaurant at 155 boulevard Saint-Germain. You'll also notice that on the left-hand side of the ceramics, the hammers have been remounted backwards.

◀ LE LUX BAR

12, rue Lepic 75018 Paris. Access: M° Pigalle or Abbesses
- Tél. : 01 46 06 05 15
- Open daily 7am-2am (from 8am on Sundays)

Only a few steps away from the famed Bar des Deux Moulins, the Lux Bar boasts some superb ceramic art from the turn of the century. Produced by the Girardoni workshop in Paris, the panel behind the counter depicts the Moulin-Rouge and the beginning of rue Lepic, with the sign for the Lux Bar appearing on top of a building in the boulevard. The other walls are also decorated by tiles with a flower motif. Slightly trendy atmosphere. Decent light French fare.

LA PETITE RENAISSANCE

36, boulevard d'Ornano 75018 Paris. Access: M° Simplon
See p. 98

AND OF COURSE ALTHOUGH THEY ARE NOT SECRET:

VAGENENDE

142, boulevard Saint-Germain 75006 Paris. Tél. : 01 43 26 68 18
- Around €25 -€30.

Handsome decor dating from 1885.

LE PETIT ZINC

11, rue Saint-Benoît 75006 Paris. Tél. : 01 42 86 61 00
- Menu: €28

Too many tourists…

LE MONTPARNASSE 1900

59, boulevard du Montparnasse 75006 Paris. Tél. : 01 45 49 19 00
- Lunch menus: €19, €26 and €32 . Evening menu: €32.

1903 decor, but a tourist trap.

LA FERMETTE MARBEUF

5, rue Marbeuf 75008 Paris. Tél. : 01 53 23 08 00

Superb decor created in 1898 by Émile Hurté, rediscovered by chance in 1978.

LE GRAND CAFÉ CAPUCINES

4, boulevard des Capucines 75009 Paris. Tél. : 01 43 12 19 00

JULIEN

16, rue du Faubourg-Saint-Denis 75010 Paris. Tél. : 01 47 70 12 06

Very beautiful 1900 decor.

LE TRAIN BLEU

Gare de Lyon - 75012 Paris. Tél. : 01 43 43 09 06

Stunning 1901 decor.

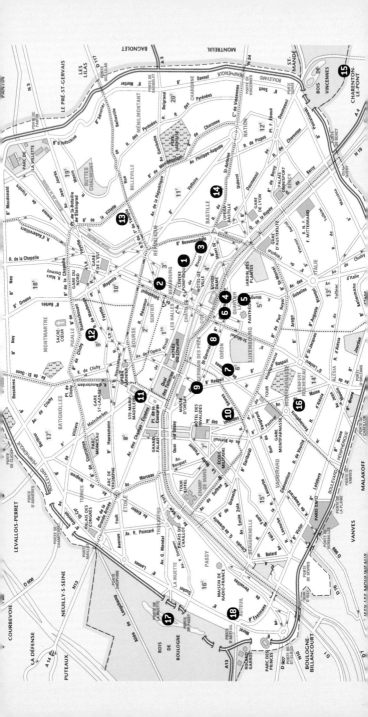

WARM FIRESIDES

GEORGET

64, rue Vieille-du-Temple 75003 Paris. Access: M° Saint-Paul
- Tél. : 01 42 78 55 89
- Around €25 per person.

In this old traditional French auberge (inn), an authentic wood fire crackles all winter long at the rear of the dining room. So try to reserve a table close to the hearth. Simple country cooking of good taste.

◄ LE QUINCAMPE

78, rue Quincampoix 75003 Paris. Tél. : 01 40 27 01 45
- Open daily until midnight, except on Sundays.

A nice bar-restaurant with a cheerful fireplace at the rear. Simple good-tasting Franco-Moroccan cuisine. Around €20.

LE PAVILLON DE LA REINE

28, place des Vosges 75004 Paris. Access: M° Chemin-Vert
- Tél. : 01 40 29 19 19
- Open daily.

This very chic hotel at the place de Vosges has a beautiful fireplace in its warm and welcoming lobby. Although this area is officially reserved to hotel guests, by asking politely you may sometimes be permitted to take tea in a comfortable sofa right in front of said fireplace.

LA FOURMI AILÉE ❹

8, rue du Fouarre 75005 Paris. Access: M° Maubert-Mutualité
- Tél. : 01 43 29 40 99
- Open daily noon-midnight.

This appealing tea-room/bookshop possesses a fireplace that crackles softly and makes reading the books available a particularly agreeable experience. Almost like being at home…

LE COUPE-CHOU ❺

11, rue Lanneau 75005 Paris . Access: M° Maubert-Mutualité
- Tél. : 01 46 33 68 69
- Open daily noon-2pm and 7pm-midnight, except on Sundays.
- Menus: €24 and €32.

Slightly too touristy, the Coupe-Chou nevertheless has a warm 18th century interior and a handsome fireplace. Traditional cuisine without surprises.

ATELIER DE MAÎTRE ALBERT

1, rue Maître-Albert 75005 Paris. Access: M° Maubert-Mutualité
- Tél. : 01 56 81 30 01
- Open weekdays noon-2.30pm, Sun-Wed 6.30pm-11.30pm, and Thurs-Sat 6.30pm-1am.

A very beautiful fireplace in a decor designed by Guy Savoy. Good but expensive, a little too noisy to be romantic, but one spends a pleasant time here, especially next to the crackling fire.

HÔTEL DE L'ABBAYE

10, rue Cassette 75006 Paris. Access: M° Saint-Sulpice
- Tél. : 01 45 44 38 11
- Open daily.

In this small but luxurious bijou hotel, it's possible to have a drink, or even a light snack (a croque-monsieur, for example), in front of the fireplace in one of the salons opposite the reception. Ideal before going to see a film at L'Arlequin cinema nearby.

CHEZ GEORGES

11, rue des Canettes 75006 Paris. Access: M° Mabillon
- Tél. : 01 43 26 79 15
- Open daily noon-2pm, except Sundays and Mondays.

Pleasant fireplace. Traditional cuisine.

LE MONTALEMBERT

3, rue Montalembert 75007 Paris. Access: M° Rue-du-Bac
- Tél. : 01 45 49 68 68

The very elegant Hôtel Montalembert has a small fireside nook that's often neglected. Take advantage of that to admire the luxury of this venue frequented by the literary folk in the neighbourhood.

LA FLAMBÉE ⑩

79, avenue de Ségur 75007 Paris. Access: M° Ségur
- Tél. 01 47 34 22 63
- Open Mon-Sat lunch time, and for dinner with reservation.
- Lunch menu: €15, dinner from €20.

In this bourgeois street, at the southern edge of the 7th arrondissement, a pleasant odour of a chimney fire greets you as you walk in the door. Everything here is cooked on a spit over a wood fire in the massive fireplace that dominates the rear of the dining room. Decorated in the manor of a Savoyard chalet, in wood and with old-fashioned skis. Friendly service and simple, frank cuisine.

1728
8, rue d'Anjou 75008 Paris. Access: M° Concorde • Tél. 01 40 17 04 77.
See p. 137

L'AUBERGE DU CLOU
30, avenue Trudaine 75009 Paris. Access: M° Pigalle • Tél. : 01 48 78 22 48
Upstairs, there's a handsome fireplace. But beware, places are hard to come by in wintertime, so make sure to specifically reserve a fireside table ahead of time.

◀ LE COIN DE VERRE
38, rue de Sambre-et-Meuse 75010 Paris. Access: M° Belleville • Tél. : 01 42 45 31 82
A very nice restaurant, simple but tasteful. At the rear, the very cheery fireplace makes one want to linger. Moderate prices, good quality, and a useful address for cold days.

LA CIPALE
51, avenue de Gravelle 75012 Paris. Access: M° Liberté ou Charenton-Ecoles
• Tél. : 01 43 75 54 53
See p. 58

LE CHINA CLUB
50, rue de Charenton 75012 Paris. Access: M° Bastille • Tél. : 01 43 43 82 02
• Open daily 7pm-2am (3am on weekends).
Upstairs, the smoking room of the famous China Club boasts a black marble fireplace that's terribly effective at producing a sense of well-being. Accompanied by a glass of port for English-speakers or cognac for the French, that quiet fireside cigar goes down smoothly.

LE BOCK DE BOHÊME
104, rue du Château 75014 Paris. Access: M° Pernety • Tél. : 01 43 22 62 96
• Open Thur-Sat 8pm-midnight.
Probably one of the only bars in Paris to possess a veritable fireplace. With a superb, softly lit ambience, lying beyond time and fashion. A rare address. Small meals available for those who forgot to have dinner.

LE CHALET DES ÎLES
14, chemin de Ceinture du Lac Inférieur 75016 Paris. Access: RER avenue Henri-Martin
• Tél. : 01 42 88 04 69
• Price: around €40.
When winter comes, the restaurant on the island of the big lake within the Bois de Boulogne is organized around a salutary fireplace that crackles pleasantly to warm your cockles.

TSÉ
78, rue d'Auteuil 750016 Paris. Access: M° Porte-d'Auteuil. • Tél. : 01 40 71 11 90
A beautiful fireplace in this trendy Asian restaurant. The few armchairs that face it are often taken by storm.

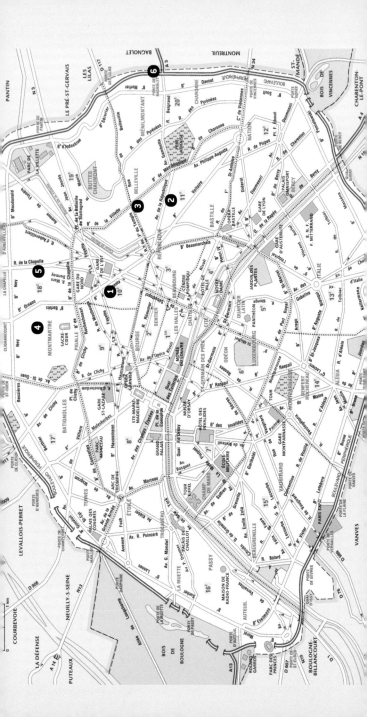

FREE FOOD

Yes indeed, it's possible to eat for free in Paris, and we're not
talking about soup kitchens for the homeless or down-and-out, either...
Most of the time, however, you'll be asked to buy a drink
to accompany the food. But don't worry, you won't even be overcharged
on the price of a beer. There are some really good deals to be had,
all the more so because of the great ambience that frequently reigns
in these places.

LES PETITES ECURIES - TRIBAL CAFÉ

3, cour des Petites-Ecuries 75010 Paris. Access: M° Château-d'Eau
- Tél. : 01 47 70 57 08

Free couscous on Friday and Saturday evenings. Mussels & chips for free on Wednesday and Thursday evenings. And with that, the owners don't even try to compensate with the rest: a demi of beer costs €2.10 and a mojito (mint rum drink) €5.50. The crowd often spills out on the pavement, but happily the street is very calm and almost free of cars.

LES FONTAINES

153, rue Saint-Maur 75011 Paris. Access: M° Parmentier
- Tél. : 01 43 57 53 14

Free couscous on Friday and Saturday evenings. Demi €2.50.

LE TAÏS

129, boulevard de Ménilmontant 75011 Paris. Access: M° Ménilmontant
- Tél. : 01 43 55 67 90

Free couscous Friday and Saturday evenings.

LA CHOPE DE CHÂTEAU-ROUGE

42, rue de Clignancourt 75018 Paris. Access: M° Château-Rouge

Free couscous Friday and Saturday evenings. A long-standing institution at this venue.

HOGGAR CAFÉ

17, rue Custine 75018 Paris. Métro Château-Rouge. Tél. : 01 42 55 93 78
Free couscous Friday and Saturday evenings

LE BAL PERDU

2, rue Charles-Graindorge 93170 Bagnolet
- Tél. : 01 43 62 93 37
- Open daily 7am-midnight.

Free couscous the last Sunday of every month. Wine €2.50, beer €2, coffee €1. Opened at the beginning of 2004 by Farid and Saïd, the owners of the Bar du Marché in Montreuil, this neighbourhood landmark in the eastern suburbs serves couscous for free to round off the last weekend of each passing month.

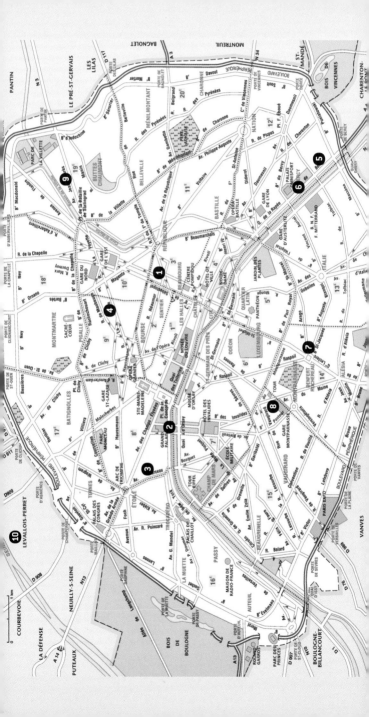

WITH CHILDREN

CAFÉ DES TECHNIQUES (MUSÉE DES ARTS ET MÉTIERS)

292, rue Saint Martin 75003 Paris. M° Arts et Métiers
• Tel.: 01 53 01 82 83 • www.arts-et-metiers.net • Sunday brunch from 11.30am

The fixed price brunch for €19.60 (€10 for 16 years and under) includes access to the museum's permanent collections. The museum offers interactive thematic workshops lasting 2hrs 30min, on Wednesdays for children only, and on Thursdays during school holidays in the Paris region for both children and parents (€4.50 per child and €6.50 per adult).

LE SHOWCASE

Pont Alexandre III, Port des Champs Élysées 75008 Paris M° Invalides
or Champs Élysées-Clémenceau
• Tel.: 01 45 61 25 43 or 06 28 28 82 88 (reservations) • www.showcase.fr
• Family brunches every Sunday, 12noon-4pm

Within the vast premises of Le Showcase on the banks of the Seine, there is a "Kids" corner reserved for children, who are looked after by a team of entertainers while parents enjoy lunch in the lounge gallery. A children's party is held once a month, and educational play activities every Sunday.

ASIAN

30, avenue George V. M° George V or Alma-Marceau
• Tel.: 01 56 89 11 00 or 01 56 89 11 06 (reservations) • www.asian.fr

An immense space devoted to Asian culture, with a totally exotic setting. Full Oriental brunch €32, under-12s €16. Original programme of activities for children, introducing them to origami (Japanese art of folding paper), calligraphy, drawing…

LE POUSSETTE CAFÉ

6, rue Pierre Sémard 75009 Paris. M° Poissonnière
• Tel.: 01 78 10 49 00 • www.lepoussettecafe.com
• Open Tuesday to Saturday 10.30am-6.30pm

A café without tobacco or alcohol, with pram park, adapted toilets, changing tables, bottle warmers and jar warmers, and nappies on sale… A calm and intimate setting with a tea salon area (€9 for a large dish + drink and baby menus at €2.20 and €4.40) and an early-learning area for infants (drawing tables, snacks corner, construction games) Activities for expectant mothers (prenatal singing), young parents (singing with baby), young children ("nursery rhymes and sensations"), and special events. Boutique for expectant mothers, babies, and young children.

CLUB MED WORLD

39, cour St Émilion, Bercy Village 75012 Paris. M° Cour St Émilion
• Tel.: 0810 810 410 • www.clubmedworld.fr

Sunday brunch from 12noon and private events (birthdays, baptisms…) bookable in advance. In the bucolic atmosphere of Bercy Village, Club Med World offers a multitude of activities for children aged 0-6 and 6-12. A very wide range of formulas are available: family brunch, children's brunch, birthday teas, flying trapeze, make-up sessions, cookery workshop…

LE CABARET PIRATE

11, quai François Mauriac (at the foot of the BNF) 75013 Paris. M° Quai de la Gare
• Tel.: 01 45 84 41 71 • www.guinguettepirate.com
• For reservations and other information, contact Amandine: petitpiratok@yahoo.fr
On a pirate ship docked at the side of the Seine, shows for children and their parents: puppets, clowns, theatre, concerts... Every Wednesday at 2.45pm (ticket office opens at 2pm). Birthday parties organised aboard ship on Wednesday and Saturday afternoons. Admission to shows: €6 per child (also unemployed, students) and €8 full rate.

◀APOLLO

3, place Denfert-Rochereau 75014 Paris. M°/RER Denfert-Rochereau
• Tel.: 01 45 38 76 77 • www.restaurant-apollo.com
• Sunday brunch 12noon-2.30pm
In the unusual setting of the former Denfert RATP/RER station, a huge space with 1970s decor, fixed-price brunch €25, children included. Storytelling and face-painting workshops all year round, Father Christmas in December, egg hunts at Easter...

LE JUSTINE
(HÔTEL MÉRIDIEN MONTPARNASSE)

19, rue du Commandant René-Mouchotte 75014 Paris. M° Montparnasse-Bienvenüe
• Tel.: 01 44 36 44 00
• Baby brunch every Sunday 12.15pm-3pm
Full brunch for €46, €23 for children. Children's space with early-learning games, child-minding by entertainers for 1hr 30min: group play, distribution of presents...

CAFÉZOÏDE

92, bis quai de la Loire 75019 Paris. M° Laumière
• Tel.: 01 42 38 26 37 • www.ateliercfd.org
• www.cafezoide.asso.fr (website created with input from children)
• Open Wednesday to Sunday 10am-7pm (including holidays unless otherwise specified)
"The first cultural café for children". On La Villette basin, the Cafézoïde is not a nursery but a real café serving children aged 0 to 16. Visual arts, theatre, music, film shows, philosophical debates... Annual membership is €2.50 (a visit is free) plus contribution to expenses (drinks, snacks) of €1.50, and €1 for large families.

LE PETIT POUCET

Île de la Jatte
4, rond-point Claude Monet. 92300 Levallois-Perret
• Tel.: 01 47 38 61 85 • www.le-petitpoucet.net
• Sunday family brunch
On the Île de la Jatte, Le Petit Poucet is a former guinguette (riverside café with a dance floor) that has been refurbished as a restaurant. Brunch every Sunday with a magic show for children 2pm-3pm (except during school holidays).

ALPHABETICAL INDEX

a. *Parc Güell (Barcelone) ?*

b. *Parc de la Villette (Paris) ?*

c. *Jardin de Tivoli (Copenhague) ?*

Vous ne savez pas quelle case cocher ?

Alors plongez-vous dans Le Guide Vert Michelin !

- tout ce qu'il faut voir et faire sur place

- les meilleurs itinéraires

- de nombreux conseils pratiques

- toutes les bonnes adresses

Le Guide Vert Michelin, l'esprit de découverte

Une meilleure façon d'avancer

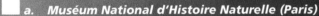

Photo Credits:
Stéphanie Rivoal except : Chez Michaël, Le Bar, Coupole du Printemps, Mollard, Cafétéria juive, Jim Haynes, Bock de Bohême, Villa Toscane, Baccarat, chez Lucette, Studio des Islettes, Noctambules, Lux Bar, Mobilhome, Ferme du Bonheur, Mains d'oeuvre : **Jacques Garance**
Procar : Bernard Cannone ; Maison d'Amérique Latine. Source : Maison d'Amérique Latine ; Aviation Club de France : source Aviation Club de France. Institut Vatel : © Institut Vatel

Cartography: Michelin - Plan de PARIS, autorisation n° 0502034, Copyright Michelin et Cie, 2005 - **Design:** Roland Deloi - **Layout:** Stéphanie Benoit - **Copy-editing/proofreading:** Caroline Lawrence - **English translation:** Tom Clegg - **Distribution:** Michelin

ISBN: 978-2-9158-0747-9

© JONGLEZ 2009